MW00325302

DAVID L. ANGERON

The Mental Training Guide for Elite Athletes

How the Mental Master Method Helps
Players, Parents, and Coaches Create
a Championship Mindset

Published by:
John Melvin Publishing, LLC
650 Poydras St.
Suite 1416
New Orleans, LA 70130
www.johnmelvinpublishing.com

ISBN: 978-1-7351627-0-6 Paperback
978-1-7351627-1-3 Kindle edition

Library of Congress Control Number: 2020910163

Illustrations by Muttley

Printed in the United States of America

This book is dedicated to the loving memory of three especially important and influential men in my life, the three Berwick High School legacies: Tommy Bourgeois, John Menard, and John Melvin.

Coach Tommy Bourgeois coached me in high school basketball, baseball, and football. He was someone who pushed me both physically and mentally to be the best player and best person I could be. I had an incredibly special bond with him, and he was one of my main influences in becoming a coach. After I graduated college, Coach Bourgeois (then the head football coach and athletic director) gave me my first coaching job as the head baseball coach and his assistant football coach in 1997. I am extremely grateful for the opportunity he gave me and the belief he had in me as a coach. Coach Bourgeois was a great motivator and one of the toughest men I ever knew. Years later he faced the ultimate adversity when he was diagnosed with ALS (Lou Gehrig's disease). Through it all, he stayed positive and continued to influence and motivate people. He lost his battle with ALS in 2014 at the young age of 55.

Coach John Menard was a good friend of mine growing up. We played basketball, baseball, and football together throughout high school and graduated together in the Berwick High School Class of 1992. In 1997, when I received my first head coaching position, John was my assistant coach. He was a dedicated and hardworking coach and helped players get better on and off the field. John later became a successful head baseball coach and then became an assistant principal. John was one of the most caring and passionate people I ever knew. John made me a better coach and a better person. In his 20 years of coaching, he touched many lives with his beautiful spirit, outgoing personality, strength, and faith. In 2019, John lost his courageous battle with cancer at the age of 44.

And John Caleb Melvin... Over my 20-plus years of coaching, I have coached thousands of players and I love each one of them as if they were my own. Being part of a team is a family bond for life. However, any coach will tell you that some players just click with you better than others. Similar personality types and certain players just gravitate toward you for guidance and improvement. John Melvin was the first player in my early coaching career that I had that special bond with. John was a little bit of a rebel, but he had an awesome, positive personality. I saw so much potential in him that I pushed him harder than I pushed the others. I became close to his parents and helped them by taking John on some of his recruiting trips. When he signed to be a Division I football player and track athlete in May of 2000, I was extremely excited and proud.

As John went on to be a two-sport athlete in college, and I moved on to begin coaching professional baseball, I continued to follow his college success. John always lived life to the fullest and could light up a room with his great smile and cheerful personality. On February 17, 2003, I received the call that his life had tragically ended in a motorcycle accident at 20 years old. I remember being devastated in my hotel room and feeling like I had just lost my brother. At that time, I wasn't sure why John had been such a special part of my life and why we had that close of a bond.

But several years later, when I returned to my hometown after my professional coaching career, I was reunited with John's family and ended up marrying John's older sister, Jean. My sports brother back then and my brother-in-law now will always be loved and missed.

All three of these small-town legacies touched so many lives. I am extremely blessed and grateful to have had them as huge parts of my life and to have learned so much from them. They all have a special place in my heart, and each of them has been influential in my coaching career and in making me the Christian family man I am today.

I hope you enjoy this book written in honor of John Melvin, John Menard, and Tommy Bourgeois.

Table of Contents

Foreword

I have a great love for sports in general and for baseball in particular. Currently, I am the co-owner of Double-A minor league baseball team the Pensacola Blue Wahoos. As a community-builder, one of my big goals was bringing this team (then called the Carolina Mudcats and located in Zebulon, NC) to Pensacola. This finally happened in 2010, and since then the Blue Wahoos have played a pivotal role in driving the city's economic development. That's the magic of baseball!

It was through baseball that I met David Angeron. We met in the pre-Wahoo days, in the summer of 2002. I had purchased a brand-new team, the Pensacola Pelicans. David had just been hired as the general manager. I saw something special in him right away. David worked around the clock to get the stadium up and running while also dealing with player recruiting and development. It was clear he was incredibly dedicated and a very hard worker, and that he had a gift for inspiring others.

I knew that when he mastered a few basic tools, he would quickly accelerate to the next level. I started coaching David on his business leadership and public speaking skills, and he took the ball and ran with it. The Pelicans went on to win the 2002 Southeastern League Championship, and from there, we started the process of making Pensacola a professional baseball town.

David and I worked together for a couple of years before he moved on to become a coach and scout at higher levels of professional baseball. Over the years, we've remained close friends.

So when David asked me to read his book, I was delighted. I loved that he was writing about the psychological aspects of playing a team sport. In getting to know many baseball players over the years, I have seen that what goes on in the mind and heart is just as important as talent or athletic ability. In fact, it may be even more important.

This is not just a "sports" thing either. It's true in business and in all areas of life.

I've had the privilege of getting to know some highly successful people from many different professions and from every industry. It's widely believed that success is about how educated or well-connected or even how smart a person is, but I have found that's not always true. Passion, drive, and resilience (which is a big part of the mental toughness David writes about) are actually far better indicators of success.

This book is written to young athletes and the coaches and parents who guide and influence them, but really, it's valuable for *all* young people. If they can master the inner game from a young age—from learning to motivate themselves, to cultivating work ethic and grit, to setting goals, to developing confidence—they'll set themselves up for success for the rest of their life.

Over the years, I've learned there are certain mindsets and habits that predictably lead to excellence and success. And as I read this book, I realized that all of them are woven into David's Mental Master Method. And he doesn't just instill these points of excellence in others. He lives them.

David is a good example of the saying that you can't take anyone else further than you can take yourself. He works on himself daily. He walks the talk, and that's what makes him a great coach and a powerful influencer. (It's also what makes him a great parent: He and his wife have raised four highly successful children, all of whom are unique individuals and strong athletes!) The mindsets and habits he embodies are the same ones he shares in this book—and they're the same ones that go into building the mental toughness that creates elite athletes.

Mental toughness doesn't just happen. The strength, resilience, and confidence required to be a great athlete and teammate—and ultimately, to excel at whatever you decide to pursue in life—don't spring up in a vacuum. All are by-products of lots of practice and preparation. I believe when you embrace the mindsets and practice the habits David writes about—the same ones that I've found through my own work consistently create great leaders and successful human beings—you build up your mental toughness.

Perhaps the most important one is this: Stay self-aware and coachable. Self-awareness just means knowing what we're good at and what we're not. Coachability means we're open to feedback from others. These are the foundations of humility, which is one of the most important traits a leader can have. David talks about them throughout this book in various ways.

Speaking of humility, it may not mean what you think. It's not about being meek or submissive or thinking you aren't good enough. It's about seeing yourself as you truly are—knowing your strengths and weaknesses. That said, it's critical to know what you do well and play to your strengths. No one is good at everything. Take what you are good at and really, really develop it.

This means you need to be willing to do the hard work. You'll find in life that there's no shortage of people with big ideas. There *is* a shortage of people who want to sit down, get focused, and put in the elbow grease it takes to execute. Be the person willing to put in the blood, sweat, and tears to get things done.

Get up and make your bed each morning. Read over the report one more time before you turn it in. Work an extra hour longer than everyone else. Be known for follow-up. Assume the ball is always in your court. Always be asking if there is anything you can do to help.

You'll see that none of the changes you're being asked to make are huge ones. Small ball matters. You don't have to knock it over the fence every time or do something grand and glorious. Often the most successful people are those who show up every day and hit a single or double, consistently.

I've found making small, incremental changes is better than making a big transformation all at once. It's more sustainable. Today and as you move through life, always be looking around to see what little, high-impact change you can make. Once you have one small win under your belt, move on to the next one. You never know where that small win might lead.

That said, never underestimate a small opportunity. Sometimes if it's not a huge contract, people don't work as hard on it. They put it off until the last minute and then rush through it. But big opportunities often grow from small ones. People watch how you do the little things before they ask you to do the big things. If you do a great job, it sets the tone for future projects.

Much of success in sports and in life is about how you treat others. Little actions and habits show people what you're made of. For instance, show up on time. It's a sign of respect and enthusiasm. And people will notice when you're late. Build in a few extra minutes just in case. (Remember the mantra *Early is on time, on time is late, and late is unacceptable.*)

Keep your promises. In fact, under-promise and over-deliver. People will be delighted when they get more than they expected, and they'll associate that feeling with you in the future.

Know that honesty and integrity matter. Deceptive or shady people can and often do thrive in the short-term. But those who are successful long-term are the ones others know they can trust and count on to tell the hard truths and do the right things (even when it's really, really hard).

When you live by these principles, you will be more likeable, and likeability is at least as important as skillset (and often more so). Don't try to be the smartest person in the room. Be interested, not interesting. Even if you really do have the best ideas, it won't matter if people don't like you enough to give you a chance to bring them to fruition.

Be partnership-oriented, not self-interested. Learn to see things from the other party's perspective. Propose ventures or solutions that are good for everybody. It is natural to seek out situations that benefit us, but successful people look for ways that everyone can win. Know that there is enough to go around. Your win doesn't mean someone else has to lose (and vice versa).

Therefore, don't be ruled by fear. Trust life. We all have fears and insecurities, but I have found that successful people refuse to let them dominate their mindset. They make the decision to see the world as a place of abundance, not scarcity. They trust that things will work out for the best and that sometimes the big pay-off comes down the road.

I did not start out knowing and believing all of these things. It has taken a lifetime. Some days I still have doubts and fears. Some days I move backward. It's okay. We are all works in progress. Every day that the sun rises, we have a chance to start over.

Finally, cultivate resilience. There are always going to be challenges for there is no utopia in work or in life. To me, resilience must go hand-in-hand with passion for your work. It's so important to select a vocation that you are passionate about, because when challenges come, both that passion and the resilience you've developed will keep you going.

You'll find David writes a lot about adversity. It's crucial that we get back up when life knocks us down. Mindset matters, and it shows up early in life. I am watching young people with great interest these days. I predict those who set out to grow stronger, mentally and physically, during this time will thrive later.

Whatever your age, I urge you to read this book cover to cover. The simple, straightforward writing makes it easy to understand and digest. The ideas, though, are valuable to anyone of any age—from middle school to high school and beyond. Do the assessments and assignments David includes. Then read the book again. If you take it seriously, you will be amazed on your second read to find how much you have grown and improved since the first time.

Growing and improving is what life is all about. Successful people know they can always be better—better athletes, yes, but also better students, employees, partners, friends, and leaders. They know they can always learn from others. They know that every day is an opportunity to grow. I hope you'll take this opportunity and run with it.

—Quint Studer
Author of *Building a Vibrant Community* and *Wall Street Journal* bestseller *The Busy Leader's Handbook*
Co-Owner, Pensacola Blue Wahoos

Introduction

I have been an athlete all my life, and I have coached athletes for the past 20 years. Here's what I have learned during this time: The single biggest factor in determining success in sports and in life is mental toughness. That's right, *mental* toughness. Elite athletes go far beyond the physical conditioning and training that their sport demands. They also master the mental side of competition, and this is what helps them rise above the rest.

In *The Mental Training Guide for Elite Athletes*, I am going to teach you the routines and exercises that great athletes use to take their performance to the next level—whether "next level" for you means making the team for the first time, or moving up to varsity, or being offered your first professional contract. When you practice these regularly and incorporate them into your life, you will be able to set and exceed goals and eventually reach your true potential.

How Athletes, Coaches, and Parents Can Use This Book

Athletes, coaches, and parents alike will benefit from this book. Athletes, you will learn strategies to make you mentally tough enough to overcome the adversity that comes along with playing sports. Coaches, you will learn all about sport psychology and can immediately begin using the exercises and techniques you learn in practices with your teams. Parents, you will learn how to best support your athlete on and off the field. By better understanding what they are going through, you can encourage them to use the strategies laid out in the book to improve their performance. Plus, you can try some of the tactics in your own life and benefit from the knowledge you learn.

Athletes

Resist the urge to speed read your way through this book. Go slowly, absorb the information, and take it to heart. When you do this, you will discover who you are as an athlete and how to best utilize these proven techniques.

Every chapter in this book is a different piece of the puzzle, and the content builds upon itself. Read it from beginning to end. Once you have finished the book and completed all of the exercises, you will have a clear picture of what you need to do in order to reach your athletic potential. The first four chapters have very important questions for you to ponder and answer. Go ahead and mark up your book by circling the results. Take notes in the margins and use the extra paper at the end of each chapter.

At the end of every chapter is a "chapter work-up" with questions or exercises. These are important as they will create your final Mental Master Method. Be sure to complete each chapter work-up. Doing only half of them won't work; only 100 percent effort will reap rewards.

Coaches

Many chapters ahead are filled with personal coaching stories to inspire and relay the struggles and successes that led me to embrace sport psychology. The message I want you to remember above all others is through sport psychology, all athletes, regardless of talent, circumstances, or lack of ambition, can become great players.

By following along in the book as the athlete would, you will discover not only how sport psychology works for you, but also how to best coach each of your players (because each player is unique, and not all strategies work for all players). Why not have the best team possible?

Each chapter has a "coach tip" section where you can take the information in the chapter and apply it to your job as a coach, but also for your own use. Showing your players how you practice and live these techniques is extremely important in getting players' buy-in.

Parents

Being a parent is much like the job of a coach, and you can work with each player to help them become the best they can be. Whether you're an athlete or not, your athlete learns and emulates what they see you do. They see your actions, whether you follow through, and how you deal with adversity. This book helps you recognize these elements in your life and gives you simple daily activities that will help you live your words of wisdom for your kids out loud in your own life. Inspire your athlete and use this book like they will: every day and with purpose.

Each chapter has a "parent tip" section where the information is distilled down for you, speaking directly to your role as a parent, and sharing how you can support your athlete's goal of becoming an elite athlete.

While reading the book, go ahead and dive into answering the questions by substituting "athlete" with "creator" or "employee" as it relates to your career. This way, you can use the techniques and work alongside your athlete. Not only will you benefit from the endeavor, your athlete will see your efforts, see the positive changes you are making, and will be more invested. Actions do speak louder than words, especially in parenting.

Now, let's get started!

CHAPTER ONE

My "Chicken Poop" Moment

"Positive thinking is more than just a tagline. It changes the way we behave. And I firmly believe that when I am positive, it not only makes me better, but it also makes those around me better."
—Harvey Mackay

"Don't worry about it, Coach; you can't make chicken salad out of chicken poop." That was the first thing I remember hearing after my first season as a coach. (The person who said it actually used a different word that I won't repeat here, since this is a family-friendly book!) That quote alone changed my entire coaching style and philosophy. That one quote is what helped me turn hundreds and hundreds of young athletes into successful men in sports, business, and in life.

The Rookie Coach

It was 1997. I was a confident, fresh-out-of-college 22-year-old who had just received my first high school base-ball coaching job. My dream job! Was I ready? Heck yeah, I was. I have played baseball since I was five years old and went on to play at the college level. I knew all about the X's and O's of baseball. What could possibly go wrong?

> *I knew all about the X's and O's of baseball. What could possibly go wrong?*

At the first athletic booster club meeting of the school year, they introduced me as the new head baseball coach. After the meeting, I had several of the longtime supporters come to me and tell me that they expected the next few years to be down since they had lost a very talented senior class last year, and the underclassmen didn't show much prom-ise. The boosters didn't seem to have much confidence in this year's athletes or the new "young" baseball coach. What they didn't realize was this cocky 22-year-old was deter-mined to be the best coach ever. I was going to prove to ev-eryone that I was not too young to be a successful head coach.

First, I put a serious off-season training plan in place. Each day for two hours after school, the players did weight training and physical conditioning, followed by individual baseball drills. One thing was certain: We would be in great physical shape.

As spring rolled around, I was determined to be the hardest working team in the state. We were physically strong, we had 10 senior players with some playing experience, and we worked extremely hard in the weight room and on the practice field.

The first part of the season was exciting. We had a new coach, positive energy, an exciting atmosphere in the stands, and the team was playing well. Halfway through the season, we had a record of 12 wins and 4 losses, and we were well on our way to breaking the school's home run record. That's when things went south.

Taking a Turn for the Worse

In the next few weeks, our best three hitters went into a slump, our pitchers started losing control, and our defense started making errors frequently. Just like that, the team was falling apart. I would get frustrated and yell at them. I would add extra conditioning for player mistakes. We would stay late and practice for four hours after school. The more I felt like I was trying to motivate and discipline them, the worse they played. We ended the season with 16 wins and 16 losses, placing third in our conference and losing in the first round of the playoffs.

> ### The more I felt like I was trying to motivate and discipline them, the worse they played.

And that's when it happened. After the playoff game, a man from the booster club meeting came down from the stands. He shook my hand, patted me on the back, looked me in the eyes, and said, "Don't worry about it, Coach; you can't make chicken salad out of chicken poop." As he walked off, I remember feeling angry for two reasons. My first thought was, *I think he just called my team "chicken poop."* Second, I never like it when anyone tells me that I *can't*. I don't believe in the word *can't*. As an athlete, if anyone said to me that I could not do something, you better believe I took that as a challenge and did everything in my power to prove them wrong. And that was not about to change once I became a coach. I quickly realized that I had to figure out precisely what he was talking about if I was going to succeed. My challenge was to learn how to "make chicken salad out of chicken poop."

My challenge was to learn how to "make chicken salad out of chicken poop."

I didn't sleep at all the night after the playoff loss. I replayed the entire season over and over in my head trying to figure out just what happened. As I looked back, I admitted to myself that our team didn't have a lot of raw talent. Our 10 "experienced" seniors had only junior varsity experience before their senior season, and none of them ever hit over .280. We didn't have a pitcher who could throw harder than 78 MPH. However, at the beginning of the season, they had played like big leaguers. *What changed?* I wondered.

My Aha! Moment

That's when it hit me. At the beginning of the season, there was positive energy and a new, confident coach who believed in his players and had helped them believe in themselves. They played confidently through the first half of the season. Then it all changed when adversity hit. The players started to lose confidence and mental focus. That's when I realized that the term "chicken poop" did not refer to my team's physical ability. The real "chicken poop" was all the negativity taking place in the players' minds. Stress, fear, doubt, anxiety, and negativity are all examples of mental weakness, a.k.a. "chicken poop."

That's when I realized that the term "chicken poop" did not refer to my team's physical ability. The real "chicken poop" was all the negativity taking place in the players' minds.

So, to prove the man from the booster meeting wrong, I needed to learn how to mentally train my players. I needed to get them mentally tough and teach them how to turn the negativity in their heads into positive energy and self-confidence. It came down to doing the research and finding the right recipe and ingredients for mental toughness, a.k.a. "chicken salad."

Here's what players and coaches alike should take away from this: When a team that is physically fit and has been performing well experiences a sudden or gradual downturn in effort, ability, and attitude, you must consider the possibility that the mental aspect could be the cause.

You must consider the possibility that the mental aspect could be the cause.

While it still doesn't get to the root of the problem, some coaches try to remedy this downturn by making the athletes work harder. They keep them at practice longer, which in turn pulls the athletes' focus back to the sport through time consumption and exhaustion. This type of coaching has its place; however, it can result in injuries and lack of energy for games, especially mid- to late season.

Turning to sport psychology as a quick-fix is not the solution either. Reversing a downturn and sustaining a winning performance takes training, preparation, and consistent daily, weekly, yearly activity and investment by everyone: coaches, athletes, and parents or caretakers. Just as an athlete does push-ups every day to stay in shape and goes through drills at practice, the brain needs its workout and daily practice, too.

Just as an athlete does push-ups every day to stay in shape and goes through drills at practice, the brain needs its workout and daily practice, too.

Physical strength and proficiency matter a lot. But these factors can take you only so far. I wrote this book to address the other side of the coin, which is mastery of your mind. You may be the biggest, the strongest, and the most naturally talented athlete, but without a strong mental approach to your sport, you can't achieve peak performance. The Mental Master Method is a plan of action that guides athletes to not only reach, but to exceed their goals and potential. It is also a lifestyle characterized by an optimistic and resilient mindset—one that prepares you to change obstacles into opportunities.

You may be the biggest, the strongest, and the most naturally talented athlete, but without a strong mental approach to your sport, you can't achieve peak performance.

In other words, the Mental Master Method teaches you to condition your brain as well as your body. In the coming chapters, I will share with you the tools, skills, and routines that help you endure and rise above adversity. You will learn powerful self-examination techniques that allow you to recognize areas of your performance and your mindset that need work. Additionally, you will learn the skills that help you perform well under pressure, work hard to achieve your goals, and create the career you dream of, no matter where you are starting from today. The examples in this book are based on my experience as a professional baseball coach and scout; however, the Mental Master Method can relate to and be effective for all kinds of athletes, performers, and business leaders—or anyone who wants to become a stronger person.

> *The Mental Master Method can relate to and be effective for all kinds of athletes, performers, and business leaders—or anyone who wants to become a stronger person.*

Where Do You Want to Go from Here?

When you practice the mental side of your athleticism as regularly as you practice for your sport, you can become not just a great athlete, but an elite athlete. Just as becoming physically fit now serves you when you're older by giving you strong bones and muscle memory, mental fitness increases your success in your career and in personal relationships from now on. It guides you when life deals you tragedy or misfortune, giving you access to a higher purpose and strength that helps you win the game of life.

Are you looking to grow from where you are currently? If you're serious about having fun while playing your sport, advancing, and even making a career out of it, I cannot stress enough how important it is that you read this entire book and implement everything you learn, every day. And I do mean *every day*. There isn't a day when you shouldn't wake up and tell yourself: *This is my day. I'm going to make it amazing.*

> ### *There isn't a day when you shouldn't wake up and tell yourself:* This is my day. I'm going to make it amazing.

Athletes, go ahead and read the *Coach Tips* and *Parent Tips* in each chapter as well so you can see what you and your sport look like to these pivotal players in your journey. It's my hope that what you read will help you understand their actions and enable you to speak to them about your thoughts and needs.

A Message for Coaches...

At the end of each chapter, there's a *Coach Tips* section. It is incredibly important that you implement everything taught here. The more your athletes can see that you are invested in the mental side of the game, the more you'll see them buy in and improve exponentially. You will witness a massive change in their attitudes, motivation, focus, and mental toughness. Imagine when all of your athletes shake off mistakes and turn around the next minute to bust out a smart play. Think about how you'll be able to focus on your job better when your athletes are so self-motivated they take the initiative to improve themselves, not hang their heads in defeat after a bad game.

I strongly suggest you read everything the athlete is learning and practice it for yourself. We can all use the tips shared in this book. Think about how this will change your game, your coaching, and your results for the better.

A Message for Parents...

Every day, you contribute to your child's athletic career. I can't stress enough how necessary it is for you to read this book cover-to-cover. Pay close attention to the *Parent Tips* sections at the end of each chapter and do your part by following the advice. You can wield a great deal of power for good or bad. Practice being a good listener, a positive motivator, and know when to step aside and let your athlete struggle to work out their own solutions. In this way, they own their success and gain the prize of true self-confidence that will carry them to a career as an elite athlete.

A Message for Athletes...

Athletes: This is very important, so pay attention! To get everything out of this book that you need to gain the edge over your competition and be the best athlete you can be, you must commit to reading and doing the work. Engage fully in the *Chapter Work-Ups* at the end of every chapter; otherwise, you'll read it and forget it. You don't want to go back to your usual mode of not understanding why you can't overcome your focus issue.

Finally, a word about how this book is structured. I have divided it into two parts. The first part (Chapters 1-6) is about learning who you are as a person and a player. This is vitally important because you won't be able to implement the techniques taught in this book without knowing who you are and how to best work with yourself.

The second part of this book (Chapters 7-15) is filled with ingredients that can transform you into a powerful athlete and person who is unstoppable in the face of adversity.

Let me tell you this now: This isn't a library book. Mark it up. Scribble in the margins, underline points that speak directly to you, and take additional notes in a separate notebook. Write down portions that resonate and hang them in your bedroom, on the refrigerator door, in your car, and anywhere that you will see them often.

What you will be learning is meant for everyday practice and implementation. As much as you work out physically, double your efforts to work out your mind. That's where winning starts—no exceptions!

As much as you work out physically, double your efforts to work out your mind. That's where winning starts —no exceptions!

Chapter Work-Up: A Dedication Pledge

There's no easy way to achieve real success in life and no easy road to becoming an elite athlete. You'll face bumps and hit roadblocks no matter what. You might as well have the tools ready to use in your toolbox right now. They will help you bounce back after defeats and know precisely where to go as soon as you get up and dust yourself off.

Dedicate yourself right now to reading this entire book. Promise yourself that you will read, at the very minimum, one chapter a day for 15 days, and read more if you can. At the end of this chapter, you will see a signature line and a place for you to put your full name and the date. By signing, you are committing to read this book entirely, take notes, take part in the exercises, and take time to make goals for yourself.

Take this seriously. This has everything to do with how you will perform in your next game. Do you want to be the person who lost their team the game with a bad play? Or, do you want to be the person who is already working on next week's game—the player who's not worried about what was, but is excited about what will be next? Quarterback Patrick Mahomes—who actually started out playing baseball—is a prime example. Known for his earnestness and upbeat attitude, Mahomes always looks to the future. It is surely this mindset that allowed him to play a pivotal role in Kansas City's late-in-the-game comeback to defeat San Francisco in the 2020 Super Bowl. Can you imagine how freeing it would be to adopt this optimism and drive for yourself? Let's beat expectations by reading two chapters today.

Sign below, make the commitment, date it, then turn this page and let's make some chicken salad.

Signature _____

Date _____

PERFORMANCE JOURNAL

CHAPTER TWO

Ingredients for Chicken Salad

"Nothing can stop the person with the right mental attitude from achieving their goal; nothing on earth can help the one with the wrong mental attitude."
—Thomas Jefferson

The next season was going to be a challenging one. The new class was even weaker physically than the previous year's class. However, unlike last year, this off-season I did not focus 100 percent on physical training. As I started to do research on the psychology side of sports, I came across this famous quote from Yogi Berra, "Baseball is 90 percent mental, and the other half is physical." Instead of spending hours after school in the weight room and conditioning, I decided I would cut the team's conditioning time down by half.

I focused the rest on developing a plan for the mental side of the game.

I came across this famous quote from Yogi Berra, "Baseball is 90 percent mental, and the other half is physical."

I spent hours and hours each day thinking of all the things that were missing from last year's squad. We ended up breaking the school home run record the previous year, so I knew the team did not lack physical strength. I made notes of everything that had happened during the season. Then I compared their performance from the beginning of the season, when they played like superstars, to the end of the season, when they played like Little Leaguers. Those notes turned into topics for research. That research revealed the ingredients necessary to build elite athletic performance.

It All Starts With Desire

The first thing missing from last year's team was ingredient number one: *desire.* Desire is a strong feeling of wanting to have something or wishing for something to happen. Later in this book, we will take desire a step further and discuss the difference in "wants" and "needs." For now, suffice it to say that at the beginning of the season, when things were going well and everything was exciting, it was easy to see the players wanted to be there.

As the season went on and we faced a little adversity, however, they seemed to lose their desire. Seniors started worrying about prom and graduation, while the underclassmen were more interested in spring break and summer vacations than they were in improving their game.

Soon thereafter, I became more aware of the changes that were occurring in the players and in the team as a whole. Once desire was gone, work ethic seemed to follow. Players who used to stay late to get in extra work were now the first ones to pack up and leave. The players' personalities began to clash, and the team started to argue and bicker among themselves. Their confidence decreased as soon as they faced a little bit of adversity.

Once desire was gone, work ethic seemed to follow.

Soon it became clear that they had lost not only their mental toughness but their physical toughness as well. Injuries began to pile up, and excuses became regular. The change in the players—from the first half of the season when everything was high energy and positive to the end of the season when they folded to adversity—was unbelievable.

As I mentioned in the previous chapter, our first season ended in the first round of the playoffs. Sure, we had achieved some early success, but in the end, the mounting frustrations and challenges of the year had won out. I knew we could do better—even become champions—and I was determined to take my players to the top! Although the team and I clearly had a long journey ahead, I had faith that I could teach them the tools and skills that would make them perform at their highest level. But first I had to learn those secrets myself...

I had faith that I could teach them the tools and skills that would make them perform at their highest level. But first I had to learn those secrets myself...

For the next several years, I studied sport psychology. I vowed to educate my players more on the mental side of the game. Learning about sport psychology and interventions has been a complete game changer in my coaching career. Using these mental training techniques, I have seen average athletes excel far beyond their initial abilities. I have witnessed below-average teams win championships. Mental training has not only helped many of my players succeed on the athletic fields but also in life as successful adults, spouses, and parents.

Mental training has not only helped many of my players succeed on the athletic fields but also in life as successful adults, spouses, and parents.

The Incredible Power of Goal-Setting

I have found that the best athletes are clear about their immediate goals and can identify all the steps required to obtain their long-term goals. From a general point of view, goal-setting seems easy. In reality, it shouldn't be taken lightly; it's not something you whip out in one session. Goals are a living, breathing part of you.

It is hard to find motivation when your goal is something generic like, *I want to be able to do 50 pull-ups by March.* Rather, you discover motivation when your goals are well-thought-out and when they mean something to you. For instance: *I want to be able to do 50 pull-ups by March, because there's a contest raising money for a children's hospital based on how many pull-ups I can do. I want to prove to myself I can mentally and physically accomplish something that means something to me.* We get into details on goal-setting in Chapter 5.

> **You discover motivation when your goals are well-thought-out and when they mean something to you.**

Visualize a Better Outcome

It's important to reflect on your performance and look to improve it. Play back the performance in your mind, then see the correction play out by envisioning a new scenario. Think of it as self-induced day-dreaming. Close your eyes if it helps. Go slowly and correct the moment. If what you're trying to fix is a recurring issue, be sure to add it to your list of goals—to tackle the tendency and replace it with a positive one. Playing back performances and visualizing corrections is detailed more in Chapter 13.

Know Yourself

Create a habit of thinking critically, examining yourself both mentally and physically regarding how you're doing and how you can do it better. Self-evaluation is imperative and can seem difficult to focus on, especially if you're not used to it. Add this habit to your list of goals. With any long-term goal, also list the short-term goals that will get you there—all those small steps to reach the creation of a new and better habit. Chapter 4 goes into more detail about discovering who you are and how best to tackle challenges and create goals based on your athletic personality type.

Sharpen Your Focus

Your focus needs to be unwavering. This means that your thoughts are locked on your goals. Reminders make this quest easier. Place inspiring quotes and specific goals in your room, in the car, in your notebooks, on mirrors, even above the toilet. You'll discover the reminders will sink into your brain, and soon you'll find yourself at practice and the quote will pop into your mind right when you need it most. This simple recall will motivate you to push through in the moment. We call this getting "in the zone." The ability to tap into the zone is what great athletes are able to do anytime, anywhere. In Chapter 11, you'll learn even more about how to get in the zone so you're at peak performance.

Place inspiring quotes and specific goals in your room, in the car, in your notebooks, on mirrors, even above the toilet.

Create a Positive Mindset

Lastly, a positive mindset must be your number-one priority every day. Your thoughts create feelings. Feelings will create moments in your day that lead to emotions that can control you. Don't let anything control you, but *you*. Control your thoughts, and you control your life and its outcome. When you do this, every obstacle becomes an opportunity, and you feel the excitement in your bones. This carries into your time on the field and off, and it is the key to being a successful athlete. Toward the end of the book, you'll learn more about how powerful positive thinking is and how it can change your game immediately.

Don't let anything control you, but **you.**

Put It All Together: The Mental Master Method

I created the Mental Master Method in hopes that you will make it your own. That means you will generate a plan specific to you, a well-honed system that you implement daily without fail. All you have to tackle and work on is yourself, and your thoughts, in order to be successful at using your Mental Master Method. It will guide you to be an elite athlete ready to flex your brain and body muscles to beat any opponent—and keep in mind that your biggest opponent just so happens to be you!

All you have to tackle and work on is yourself, and your thoughts, in order to be successful at using your Mental Master Method.

An effective method breaks down your game-day preparations into small segments that include easy mental and physical routines. Each mental routine and memorized phrase that guides you to be confident and ready for the next pitch is your Mental Master Method at work.

It's finally time to stop letting game situations and outside influences rob you of the talent you bring to the field by pressuring you, distracting you, and taking you out of the game. Put your abilities into action by using your Mental Master Method. I will teach you step-by-step in this book.

You will face adversity and not always win, but you will always be competing, and that's a real success. The more structure your system has, the more robust and detailed, the more freedom you will experience. It may sound like the opposite would be true, but a thorough Mental Master Method is your ticket to feeling confident and free when you compete. Imagine achieving your best at every moment because you put in the work that enables you to play one pitch at a time.

The more structure your system has, the more robust and detailed, the more freedom you will experience.

In these next several chapters, I am going to share with you the recipe to make the most out of negative situations. By understanding these key ingredients and how to manage and control them, you will be able to make chicken salad out of chicken poop.

Desire, goal-setting, understanding personalities, confidence, mental toughness, physical toughness, managing nerves and emotions, visualization, positive self-talk, breathing, and positive energy are all the necessary ingredients to help you become a mental master. We've talked a little about some of these already, and we will cover them in more detail as we progress through the book. Of course, you can get by with just a few of these, but to truly be a consistent and elite performer, I recommend learning how to use and control all of them.

Be sure to take notes throughout the book. It will be an invaluable resource to refer back to during the season or whenever specific situations emerge. Now, let's dive into developing a championship mindset and teach you how to make your very own chicken salad.

Coach Tip:

For sport psychology to work, your athletes need to trust you as their leader and coach. Their trust will likely come naturally at first, because young people tend to trust most adults in a teaching role. After some time, though, much trust will need to be earned. To earn trust, you need to be consistent, never show favoritism, be open to listening to your athletes, and show them respect.

To earn trust, you need to be
consistent, never show favoritism,
be open to listening to your athletes,
and show them respect.

If you don't like how an athlete is speaking to you, calmly talk to them about how you would like them to communicate to you. Most young athletes are unaware they are speaking too aggressively, too loudly, or with impatience. Show them how to get your attention ("hey, Coach") and tell them how you like to be spoken to.

Parent Tip:

To help your athlete get the most out of using sport psychology, do your homework first. Go through each of the chapters and do the exercises yourself. For maximum understanding, answer the questions for both yourself and your child.

Compare notes with your child after they have completed the questions. Give them ample time to think about who they are, what their goals are, and how they would like to move forward using all of the information they learned in this book. Lots of athletes as kids are energetic and get their thinking done while being active. Encourage them to take a run and contemplate everything. Afterward, ask them how they are best motivated, especially in regards to how you interact with them.

For example, if you tend to be a bit pushy about your athlete having a smile on their face and a cheerful attitude, this could shut down a kid who likes to be more serious. Having a scowl on their face may only mean they are focused, not upset. Get to know your kid by asking questions and listening.

Chapter Work-Up:

Before we go any further, let's start creating a plan toward your own Mental Master Method ingredients. Fill out the following questionnaire:

WHY DO YOU PLAY SPORTS? Please write out five reasons below:

1. _____

2. _____

3. _____

4. _____

5. _____

WHAT TYPE OF PLAYER DO YOU WANT TO BE? This is a particularly important question, because your answer gives direction on the next steps in this book.

_____

_____

_____

_____

_____

_____

WHAT ARE YOUR STRENGTHS?

_____

_____

_____

_____

_____

_____

WHAT ARE SOME THINGS YOU NEED IMPROVEMENT ON?

_____

_____

_____

_____

_____

_____

Complete this section **NOW**.	Complete this section **AFTER** you finish reading this book.
WHO ARE YOU TODAY?	**WHO IS THE NEW YOU?**
TODAY IS _____ (Date) AND _____ _____ (Your Name) IS AN ATHLETE WHO:	TODAY IS _____ (Date) AND _____ _____ (Your Name) IS AN ATHLETE WHO:
In this section, identify your current mental and physical strengths, weaknesses, and characteristics.	In this section, identify the athlete you want to become.

PERFORMANCE JOURNAL

CHAPTER THREE

Desire

"Desire is the most important factor in the success of any athlete."
—Bill Shoemaker

I would like to add something to the quote above: *It's up to the athlete to create that desire.* You can't take a pill to create desire, nor is it something you're either born with or not. Desire is cultivated, created through effort and daily training of your mind. Coaches and parents can help lay the foundation for creating desire, but, ultimately, it's on the player.

Have you ever been asked by a coach, "How bad do you want this?" It's a common question used to motivate athletes and teams to get them in the mode to win. We all want to win, so how does this question apply to you? Let's dig deeper and get to the heart of what Bill Shoemaker means when he says desire is the most crucial tool for success.

You would think a great swing or quick reflexes would be the most-needed asset for your upcoming competition. But as we're learning here, it's a mental game, and desire is what launches you to success—not a skill or talent that your opponent also happens to possess. What sets you apart from everyone else is that burning inside your chest that makes you unstoppable. The real question is, how do you get that burning, that desire to push hard to meet a goal?

> *Desire is what launches you to success—not a skill or talent that your opponent also happens to possess.*

"Wanting" Is Not Enough

Every year I asked my players to raise their hands if they wanted to win a championship. Of course, everyone raised their hand. Next, I asked who wanted to be a successful athlete. Again, they all raised their hands. And finally, I asked them to raise their hands if they wanted to play college sports or professional sports. Most of them kept their hands up. That's when I told them, "I want to win the lottery. I want a Ferrari." It was then that they started to get my point.

I learned a long time ago that you don't always get what you want...but you do get what you need. When you need something, you won't quit until you get it. Here's an example: When you're hungry, you always find a way to get something to eat. And when you're thirsty, you find a way to get something to drink. We're all driven like this, because food and water are needed to survive. When you can change wanting to win to needing to win, you will work harder to find a way to accomplish the goal.

When you can change wanting to win to needing to win, you will work harder to find a way to accomplish the goal.

But remember, just raising your hand or saying aloud that you need to win may not stir up the flames of desire. Unless you find the source of your desire and stoke it like hot embers in a fire, it will elude you. Once you find it, you must fan the flames of desire and help them grow. Let's go through a couple of exercises to learn how to find and nurture that desire. Then you can tap into that feeling exactly when you need it most.

First, it's essential to identify what kind of athlete you are and work from there to build your desire. The quiz below will help you do just that. And don't worry—there is no "good" or "bad" type of athlete; the only wrong answer is the one that's not really yours, so be truthful with yourself.

What Type of Athlete Are You?

Answer the following questions honestly to determine which type you are to learn how best to move forward to become a mental master. Pick the answer that best applies to you.

1. Do you pick up and play a new sport easily?
   a. Any new sport or game I play comes easily to me, so I don't always look forward to practicing it over and over again.
   b. It's sometimes easy; other times, my body doesn't always do what I want it to, or I don't understand everything right away. Still, I know that if I keep trying, I'll get better after more practice.

c. I have to work hard to get better at a new sport, and I get frustrated easily.

d. Any new sport or game I play comes easily to me, and I'm eager to learn and practice more so I can get even better.

2. Do you get anxious if you're running late for practice or if you make a mistake?

a. Not really. They can wait for me.

b. Absolutely! I get really frustrated.

c. I don't like running late, but it just happens sometimes, and it's not like I'll be missed.

d. I don't like it because I don't want to miss the action.

3. When you lose, are you upset?

a. Sure. I don't like it, but as long as I looked good and did my job, I'm good.

b. Darn right, I get upset.

c. Losing is part of playing a game, and others seem to be more upset than I am.

d. I really hate to lose, and I can be upset for a while.

If you answered mostly:

A: You are Talented but Not Ambitious.

B: You are Not Talented but Ambitious.

C: You are Not Talented and Not Ambitious.

D: You are Talented and Ambitious.

No matter how you answered the questions, you can still become a top-tier athlete. Today is a new day, and we're here to help you discover what motivates you and discover your *why*.

If the quiz determined that you are **A: Talented but Not Ambitious**, you are met daily with the question: *Why do I have to practice what I'm already good at anyway?* You find that the best part of the practice is a scrimmage and letting your athletic talent shine. I bet you also find that you lack control and have to shrug your shoulders when things go wrong, right? You may notice your teammates or certain coaches don't know what to do with you when your natural talent can't beat the opponents' innate ability. The remedy lies within your thoughts.

Often, you can find the ambition to do better, and be better, within yourself. It's also known as...you guessed it, *desire.* When your natural athletic talent gets you where you want to be—until it doesn't—desire can propel you forward. To foster desire, start by remembering the feeling you had the last time you succeeded. Close your eyes, picture yourself in that moment, and seek the memory of that feeling. *Go.*

To foster desire, start by remembering the feeling you had the last time you succeeded. Close your eyes, picture yourself in that moment, and seek the memory of that feeling. Go.

The key is to practice this every day; close your eyes, imagine it, feel it. When you have your next successful moment, take a second and remind yourself to put that feeling into your memory bank. You'll need it to tap back into it later. Much like others who have less athletic talent, you have to practice, too.

If you are **B: Not Talented but Ambitious**, you're part of the most common group. It doesn't take talent to be a great athlete. Remember, your performance is 80 percent mental, 20 percent physical. It's up to you to make the most of your ambition. Your natural desire to outplay your opponent is a huge positive. Be sure to add daily mental exercises that you will learn in this book to your schedule, thereby fulfilling the athletic goals you've set for yourself. Visualization skills will give you a much-needed edge against more athletically talented opponents.

If you are **C: Not Talented and Not Ambitious**, don't give up. You are not alone, and you can move the needle on your ambitiousness. I have seen athletes go from unambitious and unengaged to fully motivated to improve and win, toppling talented athletes along the way. Because athletic performance is 80 percent mental and 20 percent physical, you have a great chance at turning yourself around. Be sure to read about the three other types of athletes and apply everything said about ambition to yourself, knowing that you too can stoke the fire of desire when you find your purpose.

If you are lacking in talent and ambition, ask yourself this: *Why am I playing sports right now?* Maybe you're from a family that demands sports participation or you attend a school that requires it. Maybe you are just trying out your sport and are unsure if you want to go "all in." Here's the good news: Regardless of your *why*, you can easily learn and practice the art of ambition and become a great athlete. Creating goals and laying out the exact steps it will take to accomplish them will be helpful to you. I will explain this process thoroughly in Chapter 5.

> *Here's the good news: Regardless of your* why, *you can easily learn and practice the art of ambition and become a great athlete.*

When you have to fulfill a duty and be part of a team—say, the school basketball team—you have a choice. You can either hate that you have to do it (and get spoken to often by your coaches and teammates about getting a better attitude) or you can choose to be part of the team and grow as a person and athlete. If you want to stretch yourself, it's your job to find the desire within you to show up and give your best. Your key to success is focusing on a positive attitude and using visualization techniques. Along with all of the other offerings listed in this book, this will create a tremendous athletic experience and may even transform you into a great athlete. It all depends on your mentality.

If you are **D: Talented and Ambitious**, it may seem you are on the top of the heap. However, your challenge is different from everyone else's. It's all about maintaining your desire, and if part of a team, ensuring you're *really* part of the team and not a solo player out to upstage your teammates. Michael Jordan is a great example. Although he could dominate a game on his own, he knew he needed Scottie Pippen and the rest of his teammates to reach his ultimate goal of winning championships. His ambition even led him to take a break from basketball and pursue a professional baseball career before returning to basketball and winning three more championships.

Remember, no matter where you landed on the talent/ambition spectrum, you're fully capable of becoming a great athlete. It comes down to tapping into the desire to be a great athlete and compete in the given sport.

Remember: Desire is the spark that lights the fire. There's no fire without desire.

Remember: Desire is the spark that lights the fire. There's no fire without desire.

To be a competitor and create a competitive spirit in yourself or others, you need desire—a noun—a *feeling*. The competitiveness is striving—a verb—an *action*. Before you physically take an *action*—like throwing a pitch—your brain activates your arm to move. But it is your strong feeling to win, your desire, that first sparks the active push to excel. Without the feeling in place, the action can't occur.

Following is a breakdown of the four categories we just discussed. Circle or highlight which description pertains to you per your previous designation. Really absorb what you read below, because these insights will feed your success. They also will help you later on in Chapter 5 when you create your goals.

A: Talented but Not Ambitious: Players who are talented but not ambitious are often the rebels of their sport or team. They just have to show up and, without having to put in much extra work, often outperform their teammates or competitors. These athletes *love* the freedom of performing well, but their lack of ambition prevents them from doing the necessary drills, routines, conditioning, and mental exercises needed to get even better and gel with others around them.

But the fact is, you can't have freedom without first setting boundaries—guidelines and goals that help you grow and improve your game. As naturally talented as you may be, you can still be defeated by someone who is both talented *and* prepared. And that makes them non-negotiable.

> *You can't have freedom without first setting boundaries—guidelines and goals that help you grow and improve your game.*

To feel better about having boundaries in place, it's best to create them for yourself. Boundaries are crucial because your real sense of freedom can be expressed only if you are disciplined. Stick to and work within the boundaries you set, and you'll see yourself gain more freedom.

Another piece of advice for the talented but unambitious: You need to stay in touch with the people in your life and have regular outside activity—this keeps you connected and wanting to compete. It's imperative you learn and practice self-motivation and doing things for others. Being part of a group and community helps you see that you are but one piece of a larger puzzle, not the entire puzzle.

To summarize: Create your own healthy boundaries, be firm in sticking to them, and push against them only for positive competition, not accolades from the crowd.

B: Not Talented but Ambitious: You love to be encouraged by others and need to maintain your ambition to feel accomplished. Ask your coaches and your teammates to show you the mechanics of the game over and over again, and keep working on it. If you do this enough, you will start improving sooner than you think. Remind yourself that you are contributing so much more than perfect physical technique. Your contribution includes positive energy, motivating others, and putting forth maximum effort. Find your freedom within the boundaries you create for yourself that will help you feel connected and valued by your teammates and community.

Remind yourself that you are contributing so much more than perfect physical technique.

C: Not Talented and Not Ambitious: If this describes you, it's time to open your mind to the possibilities of what you can do, what you can share with others, and just how far you can go. Seek out positive encouragement, enjoy the sport because it is fun, and remind yourself it is a game. Don't take it too seriously, but don't "phone it in" either. Find the balance.

Ask your coach or someone more experienced than you to give you a mission, and help you set and continually upgrade your goals to keep you motivated and looking forward. Step into the group and make a space for yourself, so you feel included. Also, give up the need for perfect physical techniques that you don't have yet. Maximum effort and a positive go-get-'em attitude can be even more valuable to you and your teammates.

> *Give up the need for perfect physical techniques that you don't have yet. Maximum effort and a positive go-get-'em attitude can be even more valuable to you and your teammates.*

Keep working daily on your mental mastery along with physical techniques. Know that your freedom comes from creating boundaries for yourself so that you can feel secure and successful.

D: Talented and Ambitious: Your mission is to maintain your ambition all the time, especially when facing adversity. Talented and ambitious types may struggle to stay focused in less than ideal circumstances. While you prefer those perfect game days when the sun is shining, the opponents are worthy, and the bleachers are full of cheering crowds, you find it challenging to focus when it's overcast, when the stands are empty, or when you're dealing with poor field conditions. You must bring your talent to every situation, no matter how imperfect. The solution lies in creating your own boundaries and strictly adhering to your

Mental Master Method so you can experience total freedom in playing your game. Remember, when you're on a team, you are not playing only for yourself but also for others. You are one piece of a larger puzzle, not the entire puzzle. Of course, if you play an individual sport such as golf or tennis, you will experience the total freedom you crave by focusing on the moment at hand and not getting thrown by any missteps that occur during your performance.

You must bring your talent to every situation, no matter how imperfect.

A Few Desire Builders

Most athletes have felt a lack of desire at one point in their careers. As an athlete, your job is to create desire daily, so what do you do when you can't seem to muster it up?

We all have feelings that get us out of bed every day. As an elite athlete, your job is to create strong, definitive feelings that make you jump out of bed, thrilled to take on the day and see what great stuff is in store. These feelings are so real and intense they energize your body, make your skin tingle, and your foot tap. Here are a few tips below. Remember that depending upon your athletic personality type, some of these will resonate more than others.

Beat the best. Don't make records, numbers, or personal bests your main focus. Don't obsess over tracking your percentage improvements. Instead, compete to win. Focus on competing and getting better every day. Yes, naturally ambitious people like to beat records. If this motivates you, that's great. But don't get so caught up in record breaking that you lose your motivation or lose sight of everything else. If you love to compete against numbers, ultimately, you must let go and let all the training you did speak for itself as you compete to win in the moment.

Don't get so caught up in record breaking that you lose your motivation or lose sight of everything else.

"I want to win!" (Make it a mantra.) Feel free to think about, talk about, and train hard for winning and beating a record. Get comfortable talking about winning. Focusing inwardly on winning along with speaking it out loud to others is especially powerful for those who are unambitious or lack desire. Write on your mirror every morning: I want to win. For ambitious types, it's good to frame your talk with: *We* want to win (ditch the "I").

Write on your mirror every morning: I want to win.

Focus on commitment. Having a limited focus on beating a number is just that—limiting. Focus instead on developing competitive skills. This emphasizes the process instead of the outcome. Give attention to the physical, mental, technical, tactical, and strategic parts of competition. Create a relentless commitment to excellence and hard work in practice, and the numbers will take care of themselves.

Win in practice. Training is so much more than getting physically fit and having a perfect pitch. Train to win in practice. You are not a winner for finishing. Go farther. Visualize yourself winning. Feel the strain of pushing past the point of comfort until you can say, "Wow, I can actually do that!" You'll now be able to tap into that during competition.

Make it a mental competition. When you're tired and you feel you've reached your physical limit, your mental game helps you push through the "pain cave" and create a champion's mindset. One of my favorite sayings is "Get comfortable feeling uncomfortable." Train your mind to compete and push through pain and adversity. Ask yourself these questions: *How does it feel to be faced with a unique situation? How does it feel to push past discomfort?* You should encounter and be able to answer both in practice.

Fight the fear. Another tip for athletes is to compete against yourself by competing against your fear. There's only fear, and it's just a thought. Your fight is simply in your mind, and that's your first job—kill the fear with self-talk, desire to win and reach goals, and always pushing through the wall of fear every time it presents itself. Say it over and over again: *Nothing can stop me. I'm unstoppable. I can do whatever I put my mind to. I win.*

> *Say it over and over again:* **Nothing can stop me. I'm unstoppable. I can do whatever I put my mind to. I win.**

Feel the achievement. Attach emotions to your goal. Feel the intensity of what it's like to achieve your goal. We'll hit more on this in Chapter 11. This outlook can be developed through a two-way process. First, you'll need to attach your strongest emotions to your goal. Attach them to achieving, winning, and being the best you can be. Those emotions, or how you feel, is what drives you to take action. The stronger the emotion, the greater the action. Think about the result if you achieved your goal. How would you feel? Try to physically feel the feeling of achievement and success as if you already have it.

How Coaches and Parents Can Create a Foundation for Desire

Athletes need to be part of something bigger than themselves. If an athlete does not play a team sport, it's important for them to have a sense of community with other athletes in the sport. Encourage them to join an athletic club or a community-based organization. But also urge your athlete to become a student of their game; the more an athlete enjoys and learns about their sport the more they fall in love with it.

Urge your athlete to become a student of their game; the more an athlete enjoys and learns about their sport the more they fall in love with it.

It is also important that athletes volunteer and donate to charities to get a sense of being part of a community, so consider participating in a team fundraiser for a worthy cause. This creates a sense of responsibility, a responsibility to compete and win, and a sense of being part of something bigger than themselves. Done as a team, it can create a sense of family. Players band together to serve others and problem-solve.

Coaches can increase desire in athletes by creating a controlled, frenetic practice. Make sure it is fast and energetic with a hint of wildness and a hint of chaotic harmony. A volleyball coach was famous for running a particular drill before games that amazed the crowd, distracted the competition, and stoked the desire of the athletes to play at their highest level. The drill was run 10 times faster than normal with several balls in motion at once. There were 12 athletes performing in action simultaneously, all of it organized by a natural rhythm the athletes fell into. They knew the space they occupied and how to work together through communication techniques, intuition, and lots of practice. Their actions were so automatic that the athletes were able to play in the moment. Nothing else mattered.

Coach Tip #1:

Coach your athletes to become great competitors. They are more than just athletes who train. Create competition in training by placing athletes in new and challenging situations. Invite a new team to compete against yours (perhaps consisting of older or younger athletes), or compete in a different sport that enhances the senses and creates competitiveness and adaptability. Ensure that the players learn from losing—never let them quit and remind them of the goal, making it the priority over everything else.

Ensure that the players learn from losing—never let them quit and remind them of the goal, making it the priority over everything else.

Coach Tip #2:

If any part of you believes that a kid who lacks desire can't become a great athlete upon discovering their desire to be the best, please change your mind right now. I have personally helped kids with no desire for baseball and medium athletic skills grow into hardcore athletes who loved the sport. If you are willing to share your love of the sport, coach the athletes (after discovering how each individual on your team is motivated), and teach your athletes the mental tools in this book, you can instill desire in your players. But because 80 percent of performance is mental and 20 percent is physical, you must watch your thinking and actions toward your athletes if you want them to succeed.

Parent Tip #1:

Often school work, jobs, or financial issues create stress for athletes, and they may take these distractions to the field. Help them set up a schedule that eliminates procrastination and stressors. When they can manage homework, afterschool jobs, and are responsible enough with money that they can meet their needs, they can leave everything else behind when they hit the field.

Parent Tip #2:

Remember, your desire is not your child's desire. They must have their own desire before pursuing athletic greatness. You can help them discover this desire within them by asking questions and listening, not by directing them or telling them what you believe is best. Let them own their desire, goals, and the pursuit of success. Ask your child to share with you the best part of the sport they are participating in. Ask them to share the part they like the least as well, and why. Don't judge what they say or try to give them advice. Ask if they want to improve and how they want to achieve this improvement. Ask if you can help, and if they say no, let them work it out themselves, trusting that the coach has got their back.

Chapter Work-Up:

It's time to create your *why.* I cannot stress enough how utterly important this activity is to your future success. If you don't have a *why*, you don't have a reason to be on the field, the track, or the court. Without a *why*, you'll hit a wall and wonder how you're going to get back up. The good news is, your *why* will not only help you up, it will show you the way. The more connected you are to why you play, the more freedom you'll experience, which empowers you to deal with frustrations the game gives you.

It's time to create your **why.**

Why do you play? What do you enjoy? When were your most fun times? Who's your ideal player? Why? What do you miss about playing when you're off-season? Let's take this step-by-step. Use the blank paper at the end of the chapter and answer the following:

1. In a few words, describe a time when you lost desire and why.
2. Now, describe a time when desire was strong.
3. Put your pen/pencil down, close your eyes, and try your best to remember what it was like to feel that desire. Picture a moment when it was high, maybe when teammates were all around you cheering before the season opener. Try to tap into that feeling you had then right now.
4. Why was your level of desire elevated during this high point? Show your ambition by using descriptive words and explain everything.
5. Take everything you've written (especially the keywords that stand out to you) and write one sentence describing why you play. Here's an example: I play baseball because I love being outside on the grass. I love that it's a team sport where we can win together, but I also love that I get to perform individually.

It's time to move on to the next chapter, where you learn more about your personality type and how best to use it to become a great athlete and a great person all-around.

PERFORMANCE JOURNAL

CHAPTER FOUR

Understanding Personality Types

*"Ability is what you're capable of doing.
Motivation determines what you do.
Attitude determines how well you do it."*
—Lou Holtz

"To know thyself is the beginning of wisdom."
—Socrates

There is no one else like you. There is no other athlete exactly like you. No matter how hard you emulate your favorite professional athlete's swing, it will never be the same. And it shouldn't be, because you bring to the game an entirely different personality, attitude, and character. This is why knowing who you are, what your strengths and weaknesses might be, is the beginning of the wisdom that will make you an elite athlete.

Your personal motivations and goals are just that—yours. Your teammates bring with them their own motivations and goals that make up their personalities. Put all those unique personalities into a team, and you can get some really interesting results. This chapter delves into basic personality traits of athletes. You will find out which one you are (or, if you're a coach, which one your players fit into) and learn to use that information as a guide to help you be a champion.

Put all those unique personalities into a team, and you can get some really interesting results.

Let's dive into personality types for athletes and what it means about you. There are no right or wrong results. Knowing your personality type simply helps you and your coach become aware of your traits and discover how best to make the most of your abilities. This is a fundamental step that will lay the groundwork for your athletic excellence.

Personality Types Explained

In this section, you will discover what makes each athlete different—and I mean very different—from one another. There are several different personality traits, but I will focus on the two main traits that I feel are most important to sports. These two main traits are extroversion and neuroticism.

Extroversion (Extrovert or Introvert). Extroversion is the extent to which an individual is comfortable in social situations. Extroverts are sociable, outgoing, and active. Introverts are much the opposite; they are often quieter and more reserved than their extroverted counterparts. The teammate who enjoys being the center of attention and likes telling stories to large groups is more extroverted, whereas the teammate who is more comfortable in one-on-one conversations and withdraws from large groups is more introverted.

There are clearly some benefits of being an extrovert in sports. The energy level brought on by extroverts can be contagious. A team needs extroverts because they bring motivation to the locker room. Most team captains are extroverts because they enjoy the role of being the center of attention and can communicate and motivate others.

However, having a team full of extroverts would not work. Introverts are an important and much-needed part of the team. Could you imagine a team full of extroverts all fighting for attention and trying to be the leader and getting upset when they can't talk over the rest of the group? Introverts consider their thoughts very carefully before they speak their mind. They think more about their own performance and less about being the center of attention.

*Could you imagine a team full of
extroverts all fighting for attention
and trying to be the leader and
getting upset when they can't talk
over the rest of the group?*

Having both extroverted and introverted players is very important to a team. Being able to identify their personality traits and properly address the needs of each individual is the challenge that many coaches struggle with.

Extroversion Recap:

Here are some qualities of an extrovert. Remember, these innate qualities are neither good nor bad. See if you recognize some of these qualities in yourself. Then think about your teammates. Who among them might be an extrovert?

- Speaks up and wants to share their ideas.
- Likes to take charge of getting stuff done and may even like to lead others.
- Gets charged-up by being with others and doesn't usually like to be alone for too long.

Now, here are some qualities of introverted types. Do any of these traits resonate within your own personality? Which of your teammates display some or all introvert traits?

- Doesn't talk as much in group settings.

- Likes to spend time alone after being in group environments to recharge.
- Doesn't like taking the lead in groups.
- Keeps their thoughts and opinions to themselves.

Neuroticism (Stable/Conscientious or Wired/Neurotic). Neuroticism describes the extent to which an individual is emotionally stable (stable/conscientious) or unstable (wired/neurotic). A teammate who is even-tempered is likely to be emotionally stable, while a teammate who tends to have mood swings trends toward the neurotic end of the continuum. By the way, while the "wired/neurotic" end of the spectrum may sound like an undesirable label, it is not meant to be harsh or judgmental. We all display, at different times and under different circumstances, degrees of each of these traits because we are human. Your power lies in learning your natural tendencies and working with them to become a better athlete.

Your power lies in learning your natural tendencies and working with them to become a better athlete.

Neuroticism is more evident in sport than in everyday life. This is due to the intensity of emotions that athletes experience during pressure situations. And sports are constantly producing pressure situations. Neurotic individuals are typically jealous, have a tendency to overreact, and often seek instant gratification, whereas stable athletes are less jealous and more level-headed.

As coaches, we all want our players to be stable and controlled. But the truth is that many of them are not. This is why proper mental training and psychology practice is so very important.

Neuroticism Recap:

Here are a few traits of a person who is stable/conscientious. Think of your teammates who display these traits. How do they support the team?

- Agreeable, coachable, works well with almost anyone.
- Likes it when everyone gets along (which brings balance but also leads to indecisiveness); doesn't easily make quick decisions and would rather go along with what the group wants.

Here are some traits of a person closer to the wired/neurotic end of the spectrum. Do you recognize any of the traits in yourself? In your teammates?

- Anxious, energetic, does things without thinking about others.
- Has an idea and will stick to it no matter what.
- Very focused, may have a lot of stress and often feels under pressure. Shows up to the game early. Often talks or finds something to do.

Personality Quiz

Now that you know a little about the personality traits that are most likely to impact your athletic performance, this quiz can help you determine your levels of extroversion and neuroticism. Answer the following honestly, based on what you would really do in the scenarios described below. This is about your gut feeling and initial reaction to the choices, so circle your answer quickly.

1. You're staying home this Saturday, and it's your only day off for the next month. Will you...
   a. Invite friends over or hang out with family for at least a couple of hours.
   b. Hang out alone the entire day.

If you chose a) circle this word: **Extrovert**
If you chose b) circle this word: **Introvert**

2. You have to take a two-hour test. You are offered one of the following choices:
   a. Take the test in the library with a couple of other people.
   b. Take the test in the cafeteria with everyone around you talking and eating, because it doesn't bother you.

If you chose a) circle this word: **Introvert**
If you chose b) circle this word: **Extrovert**

3. You're on a trip with friends to a seaside town, and you are hanging out in a huge arcade. One guy

has dominated the air hockey table for 20 minutes. Now it's your turn to try and knock him off the table and win it for yourself. You discover his trick has been to kick the table as the legs are loose. You choose to:

a. Laugh it off and play anyway because you like the extra challenge.

b. You're already mad that he's cheating. You either avoid playing him, or if you do play him, you make sure he doesn't cheat.

If you chose a) circle this word: **Stable/Conscientious**
If you chose b) circle this word: **Wired/Neurotic**

4. It's your job to take the garbage out and return the can back to the garage each week. Lately, something has been tipping over the can and making a huge mess that you have to clean up the next day. You're aggravated that this keeps happening; it stinks and you don't have the time for it. As you pick up some of the trash, a bunch of rotted dog food (or was that poop?) smears across your arm. You feel and think...

a. Upset. You need a trap.

b. Motivated. You want to figure out a good solution; maybe bungee cords will hold the lid on.

If you chose a) circle this word: **Wired/Neurotic**
If you chose b) circle this word: **Stable/Conscientious**

Again, don't worry that any of your answers make you "good" or "bad." Don't judge yourself harshly if you thought an animal trap was the best solution. And you're not weird for wanting to take a test in a silent room away from distractions. A mix of all of these traits (patience, impatience, choosing solo or social time, etc.) can sometimes depend on your mood, circumstances, environment, and so forth. And remember, with some balance and mental training, any and all traits can make up the secret sauce for being a superior athlete.

Remember, with some balance and mental training, any and all traits can make up the secret sauce for being a superior athlete.

Advice for Players, Coaches, and Parents

Now it's time to take what you've learned about your own personality and start thinking about how to work with this knowledge and how best to utilize it in sports. Coaches (and parents), you will also learn a few insights about how to best motivate and work with your athletes.

Goals for Introverts: If you are an introvert, set goals that encourage you to speak up in groups and learn to be a leader. Recently, there has been an uptick in books on introverts learning to speak up in an extroverted world, and reading these will help. Reading books on leadership may also be helpful. Make an effort to tell others your opinion and get others to join you on a project you've started.

Coaching Introverts: Yelling and pointing your finger at an introvert or making everyone look at them will not win you their loyalty, and it will never motivate them to do better. If you need to correct an introvert's performance, meet with them later and without emotions. Be logical about solutions and criticisms.

- Encourage them to speak up for themselves by reminding them that you're there to listen.
- Introverts like to be rewarded with truthful praise given one-on-one—not in front of a crowd.
- They may want to spend more time practicing or thinking about a new method or system, so give them the time they need.

- Putting a red dot on the hand so they can be visually reminded to focus on a certain aspect of the game or their performance is constructive. Encourage them to visualize the future and make big goals as this helps motivate them.

Goals for Extroverts: If you are an extrovert, be sure to set goals that encourage self-reflection. That means you need to frequently ask yourself, *How would my idea affect others?* Ideas you might want to explore also include: thinking about what others need, asking their opinion, and listening to what they have to say and considering it. These are traits and actions of a leader.

Additionally, create goals that help you consider others' needs and goals that give you time alone to think about how you're going to become an elite athlete. For you, this book is really important because it asks that you take time alone and away from other people to figure out who you are, what you want, and how to be the best. You can't do this with all your friends and teammates around you.

Coaching Extroverts:

- Extroverts like attention and listen when you speak to them directly in group settings. Raising your voice and speaking to them sternly gets them fired up and ready to perform. However, be sure to follow-up after the game with positive feedback.

- They enjoy sensory input and do well with distractions. Extroverts are the ones who fidget or bounce their knee while they're listening quietly.

- Extroverts like facts and visual aids. But don't mistake their confidence and speed for athletic competence. Again, use words to motivate them and remember that it's okay to be more intense with your tone and physical gestures.

Goals for the Stable/Conscientious: If this describes you, be sure to set goals that are based on advocating for yourself, being decisive, and sharing opinions and thoughts that might counter others. Take time to think about what's best for you and come up with good ideas that you'd like to help carry out on your team or individually as an athlete.

Coaching the Stable/Conscientious: Your challenge as a coach will be to take stable and conscientious athletes that seem to always be a 5 on a scale of 1 to 10 and push them to improve their performance.

- These athletes typically respond well to direction and will do as you say. That means you need to encourage them to make decisions, make some noise, and most of all make sure they're staying motivated. In Chapter 12, we go over motivation, with some great tips on keeping introverts and stable athletes motivated.

Goals for the Wired/Neurotic: If this describes you, set goals that are based on gaining some balance and being more flexible. Listen to others and adapt to change by using relaxation techniques. Give a lot of attention to Chapters 13 and 14 and add this to your list of goals.

Coaching the Wired/Neurotic:

- Be sure to work daily with these athletes on relaxation techniques to keep their anxiety and attention balanced.
- These athletes can obsess over one technique or choke at the last second, so be sure they have pregame and game-time techniques to keep them

balanced. Chapters 11 and 14 will be valuable resources.

It Takes ALL Traits

You'll run into many coaches and people out there who have long believed that the best athletes are extroverts who are stable and conscientious. No doubt these traits are great. These athletes are viewed as more coachable and have a positive team sport attitude. There are many instances, however, where shy, quiet, and even extremely anxious players can still make elite athletes.

Who would have thought a guy who doesn't talk much and likes to stay away from the media and spend time alone could be a successful quarterback and a top draft pick for the NFL? The Cinderella story of Justin Herbert is a great example of why you should never judge a book by its cover. Introverts *can* be leaders and play in team sports.

> *The Cinderella story of Justin Herbert is a great example of why you should never judge a book by its cover.*

In their December 4, 2019, issue, *Sports Illustrated* stated that Marcus Arroyo, then offensive coordinator for the University of Oregon Ducks, gave Herbert the book *Quiet: The Power of Introverts in a World That Can't Stop Talking*, written by Susan Cain. Interestingly, Arroyo's wife is a psychologist and suggested the book for Herbert. This is proof that any personality type and all the traits you have are malleable and can benefit your athletic pursuits.

It's also commonly accepted that only extroverts can be good at team sports, or that only coachable athletes can turn out to be great at any sport. That's false and there's proof. Again, look at how Justin Herbert proves the status quo wrong: This multi-sport athlete sacrificed premier opportunities to be seen as a prime NFL draft pick so he could finish out his basketball and baseball seasons.

What many scouts and coaches didn't see is that Herbert's multi-sport dedication showed loyalty, adaptability, and motivation—prime traits in an athlete. This was all overlooked because Herbert was introverted, liked to spend time alone, and didn't focus entirely on football. And yet he blew everyone away with his 2019 season performance, launching him into the top 10 selection for the 2020 NFL draft. There are many more examples of introverts or wired (technically neurotic) athletes overcoming perceptions of others and becoming exceptional pro athletes.

Coach Tip:

There is no cookie-cutter way to coach athletes. Every player has individual personality traits along with different strengths and weaknesses. Over the years, I have encountered many coaches who treat every player the same. However, the most successful coaches individualize their coaching styles to fit each player.

There is no cookie-cutter way to coach athletes.

In my career, I have had players I knew I could push mentally. I knew I could get fired up with them and get in their face. When those players got a little tear in their eye from being mad at me, I felt sorry for their opponent, because they were about to see them at their best.

And then I had some players I knew I could not yell at in order to get the results I wanted. Instead, I would need to be passive and pat them on the back and say it's okay. If I were to give them the same aggression I gave to the other players, these personality types would shut down.

But no matter how I handled each individual player during a negative situation, I would always go back to them within a few minutes to give them some positivity and let them all know how much I cared about them. I have seen coaches fuss at a player and send the kid to the bench and never go back to talk to that player again during the game. That is a recipe for destroying that athlete's mentality. Always go back with a kind word of encouragement, no matter which type of athlete you are working with.

Always go back with a kind word of encouragement, no matter which type of athlete you are working with.

The key to success is to take time to discover what motivates all your athletes, learn their threshold (for pain, for mental toughness, for learning new skills or habits), and get to know them by asking questions. Show them you're invested in the mental side of the game, share what you know and have learned, and how it relates to them. When you take the time to get to know each of your players individually, you'll start noticing they are more hardworking and loyal and will push themselves more in practice and in competition.

During my many years of coaching, I've witnessed coaches giving up on athletes they can't get to perform at the level of the other players. I've had coaches come up to me and say, "I can't do anything with that guy." The interesting point is they had not tried working with the athlete on their mental game. First you must discover what makes each of your players tick and then learn to implement the tools and techniques yourself. Then you may teach them to your players. Why lose a player to low ambition when they can be coached to create their own desire and ambition? They may even surprise you by becoming your best player. It's happened before.

Why lose a player to low ambition when they can be coached to create their own desire and ambition? They may even surprise you by becoming your best player.

Parent Tip:

Work alongside your athlete to discover who they are and what motivates them. Ask them first and listen to what they have to say. They might say they don't know, but keep asking them questions, especially situational questions. For example: When it's late and you want to go to bed but know you have another 30 minutes of homework to do, what would be the best way to motivate you to do it? Set a timer? Have me or someone else encourage you to get it done? Do some push-ups? Self-talk?

Work alongside your athlete to discover who they are and what motivates them.

You can also think back to when they were younger and recall how you naturally found a way to motivate them to do something. Maybe you had to speak firmly with them to gain their attention and focus because they respond to auditory stimuli. Maybe your kid needed a good laugh to get relaxed first. Discuss this with your athlete so you can find ways to use the same methods that are more appropriate for their age now.

Chapter Work-Up:

For this chapter work-up, here is another quiz to help you further identify some of your unique traits. Read through the options and quickly circle the ones most like you. Don't overthink it—go with your first gut reaction:

1. It's game day and...

    a. I'm anxiously waiting for the time to leave for the field. I cannot sit down and read. I'll happily do chores to keep me busy because I want to be there already.

    b. I consider sitting on the couch watching old games to prep for today's game. Or I might hang with my friends; it relaxes me.

    c. I have a routine set for all the game days; I don't let anyone mess with it.

2. Circle the choice that sounds most like you:

    a. When it's my turn to take out the garbage, I sometimes put it out a day early. I've put out the recycling too soon before, and it just sits there a couple of days. Better early than never.

    b. My roommate is usually the one reminding me to take out the garbage, or they just do it.

    c. If it's my week to take out the garbage, I set an alarm on my phone. Then I'll set it out that morning before I leave for the day.

Below is the answer key. Please circle and read the trait that applies to you:

Answered A: High-Strung. This trait is characterized by "big energy" that is sometimes wasted because it's erratic and based on emotions. Individuals who are high-strung don't always have a lot of forethought. The to-do list is forgotten in favor of in-the-moment distraction. Everything depends on what's going on around them, what they are thinking, and what they are feeling. Your attribute is that you are a doer; if you think it, you do it.

Answered B: Low-Key. You tend to do what you're good at and nothing more. You like to rely on others to pick up the slack. Your attribute is that you're very willing to do the work, especially when it's done with other people around to hang out with.

Answered C: Tightly Wound. For tightly wound types, schedules are your friend. Last-minute changes and unpredictable situations are not your friend. You are at your best when things are scheduled at least a couple of days in advance. It takes time for you to feel prepared. Your attribute is others can rely on you showing up on time and ready to go.

Keep these traits highlighted. You'll need to find these again at the end of the book to compile your Mental Master Method.

PERFORMANCE JOURNAL

CHAPTER FIVE

Goal-Setting

"The most important key to achieving great success is to decide upon your goal and launch, get started, take action, move."
—John Wooden

Not having goals is like playing a game without keeping score. You can't tell if you're winning or losing, and there's a lack of purpose to it all. Soon you get bored, give up, and move on to something else. Rinse and repeat. Unless you want to feel like a mouse running on a wheel every day, it's important to learn the value of setting goals and working—sometimes very hard—to reach them. In this chapter, we will learn what goals are, what kinds of goals there are, and then set some goals you can start working on right now.

A goal is anything you want to work toward—an accomplishment that will mean something to you and that (hopefully) brings you excitement whenever you think about it. You may have been asked to create goals in the past. Maybe you gave it a shot and wrote an ambitious list of aims and pursuits. But if you are like many people, it was a short-lived moment of excitement that was forgotten in the day-to-day motions of life. That's because goals are hard to define and even harder to achieve. This doesn't mean they are out of reach though. Whether this is your first go at setting goals for yourself, or your twentieth attempt, commit to living and breathing the goals that you will create for yourself today. That's the only way to reach them.

Whether this is your first go at setting goals for yourself, or your twentieth attempt, commit to living and breathing the goals that you will create for yourself today.

The best athletes have carefully refined goals. They can tell you their goals from memory because they burned them in their brains, and they are on their mind all day long. They know what it will take to reach their goals and how long it should take. They have broken down the steps needed and are clear about the direction in which they are moving. The benefit of having this sense of direction is that it takes the stress away from not knowing what's next or how to react. With well-thought-out goals, your focus becomes so clear that even the people around you know your goals, because you live them out loud every day.

With well-thought-out goals, your focus becomes so clear that even the people around you know your goals, because you live them out loud every day.

A Look at Short-Term and Long-Term Goals

Goals can be either short-term or long-term. Your short-term goals are those that keep you on track to tackling those bigger long-term goals, and they give you a boost of happiness and confidence that spurs you on toward more achievement. Short-term goals set a solid foundation, getting you to take daily, small steps, so your ultimate goal doesn't seem too far away. Another fact about short-term goals is that they can be *very* short-term—so short-term, in fact, that they are immediately attainable (e.g., doing those 30 push-ups every morning for one week and being able to do 50 push-ups by the end of two weeks).

Short-term goals set a solid foundation, getting you to take daily, small steps, so your ultimate goal doesn't seem too far away.

Long-term goals are visionary. They can take months or years to reach. That means they push you almost beyond your dreams; they get you to rocket forward and obtain what you want most.

Goals that are more long-term are made up of numerous short-term goals. An example of a long-term goal is becoming a professional athlete by the time you're 24. Something this ambitious requires you to reach lots and lots of short-term goals like doing push-ups every morning, practicing breathing techniques before you go up to bat, taking 100 extra swings in the batting cage after each practice, performing three speed training workouts each week, or throwing long toss at least three times each week. This is why short-term goals are so valuable; they are the building blocks to reaching those visionary long-term goals that you dare to dream about. And again, short-term goals are often fairly easy to achieve if you pursue them with dedication. So don't shy away from setting small, attainable goals for yourself. They add up to big achievement.

Don't shy away from setting small, attainable goals for yourself. They add up to big achievement.

Getting to Know Your Goals: Questions and Answers That Lead to Your Future

Creating goals for the first couple of times can sometimes lead to a breakthrough idea, so let's start with some questions designed to get you thinking. Write down your answers either here in the book or on a separate piece of paper. All serious athletes have gone through this process and make it part of their routine for success.

Fill in the blanks below.
What do you like most about being an athlete?

_____

_____

_____

_____

_____

I play (sport) because _____

_____

_____

_____

_____

_____

_____

I want to improve _____

_____

_____

_____

_____

_____

_____

Write down as much as you can until you have fully answered the questions above. Give yourself some time to do this. You may need to sit for a while and think about the questions before the answers begin to flow.

Now, look at your answers, consider where you are heading as an athlete, and write down a long-term goal and the short-term goals that will get you there.

Long-Term Goal: _____

_____

_____

_____

_____

_____

Short-Term Goals to Help Me Meet the Long-Term Goal: _____

_____

_____

_____

_____

_____

What you have listed above, especially under "short-term" goals, is a starting point. As you continue reading the chapter and gaining insights about your goals, don't be surprised if you come up with additional short-term goals to add to the list above. You may even decide to adjust your long-term goal as you think about what you want and where you're headed. Feel free to keep expanding this list. It's okay if it gets a little long; remember, short-term goals are the building blocks of your long-term goal.

Don't forget to include goals that strengthen you mentally. It's easy to write down physical goals, like those 30 push-ups you're going to do every morning. But the truth is, your mental goals are even more important. Your mindset and mental goals will help you feel excited about getting out of bed every morning wanting to do those push-ups, and getting yourself to 75 reps a morning. It takes training your mind to do that. Your body will follow. Take a moment to write down some goals that can give you the mental edge you need to be a superior athlete. Some examples might be to track your performance in a journal at the end of each practice or game, to practice meditation for 20 minutes at least three times a week, or to focus 100 percent on the process (not the outcomes) during a game.

Don't forget to include goals that strengthen you mentally.

Make sure that all of your goals should have you focus your time and energy on things you can control. (And don't worry; *a lot* of things are under your control.) Understanding that successful players have many of the following traits in common is key to your success: courage, honesty, dedication, mental toughness, sportsmanship, fun, unselfishness, focus, leadership, composure, concentration, pride, hard work, relentlessness, consistency, integrity, tenacity, desire to learn, respect for the game and others, confidence, love of the game, commitment, and a desire to compete.

Make sure that all of your goals should have you focus your time and energy on things you can control. (And don't worry; a lot of things are under your control.)

You may not possess all of these traits yet. Still, these can be developed, and they are great goals for which to aim. Here's an example: I want to be mentally tough, so that when I feel like I can't give anything more, I find another pocket of energy and interest in what I'm doing that propels me forward. I will never give up.

The Three Traits That Help You Achieve Your Goals

What kind of player do you want to be? From years of playing and coaching, I've found these three traits are the most important for helping you transform into a great athlete. Use these to create your goals.

1. Fun and Enjoyment

- Here's a great quote from Ken Griffey, Sr: "If you have FUN, it changes all of the PRESSURE into PLEASURE!"
- "Sometimes you have to say to yourself that you're going to have fun and feel good before you go out there. Normally, you have fun after you do well,

but I wanted to have fun before I did well, and that helped." —from Hall of Famer Dave Winfield

2. Respect for the Game

- Hall of Famer Carl Yastrzemski said the off-season prepared him mentally: "I hated to do weights. I hated to run. But I did them. I swung a lead bat and hit balls—300 to 400 a day—into a net for one reason: to toughen myself mentally."

- What was Carl Yastrzemski saying? That no matter what, he was going to do what was needed to get better so he would be one of the best in the game. Do you treat yourself with the same respect? Do you show the game the respect it deserves by doing all that you can to make yourself a better player? The very act of reading this book is making you a better player, so you're on the path already. Be proud of that.

3. Pride

- A strong sense of pride in your sport performance motivates you to prepare for each practice and game and to perform consistently at a higher level—even when you don't feel you are physically capable of giving 100 percent. If you know you are going to ask yourself when you walk off the field, *Am I proud of what I did today?* you'll probably put forth the extra effort to get the most out of that day.

If you know you are going to ask yourself when you walk off the field, Am I proud of what I did today? you'll probably put forth the extra effort to get the most out of that day.

Again, what kind of player do you want to be? I'm not asking for a generic, "I want to be a good player," or, "I want to be the best player on the team," response here. This is unique to you. If you're introverted, your long-term goal might be to learn about leadership techniques for those who are introverted. A short-term goal would be to practice speaking up when you have an idea or when you want to motivate those around you when the game isn't going well.

Making Progress on SMARTER Goals

Over the years, I've reworked my goals to move with my life as it changes. I make sure they are specific, so there's no room for letting my focus slide. Here are some additional characteristics I adhere to whenever I set goals:

- They are measurable, so I know when I have accomplished them.
- They are positive, because I want positive results.
- They are written using positive words that help me stay motivated to stick to them.

- They are challenging, as they need to push me to be better, instead of keeping me at the same level.
- They are adjustable, because as my roles change, teams change, and jobs change, my goals need to move with me.

I urge you to establish a vision of what setting and achieving goals looks like to you. Make sure the long-term and corresponding short-term goals that you add to your list are very specific and measurable. Why? Because you need to visit your goals often and feel you are making progress. The very act of doing the work of obtaining your goals every day for two months is in itself meeting a goal. Using SMARTER goals can help you along the way.

I urge you to establish a vision of what setting and achieving goals looks like to you.

Maybe you've heard of SMART or SMARTER goals before. The popular business acronym SMART first appeared courtesy of George T. Doran in a November 1981 issue of *Management Review*. SMART describes the characteristics that surround achievable goals; they should always be Specific, Measurable, Achievable, Relevant, and Time-bound. Over the years, this acronym has since been adapted further by many experts and leaders, and today it is sometimes referred to as SMARTER goals. I have made a few adaptations of my own, and the results are in the following chart. Check it to learn about SMARTER goal-setting and refer back to it as you keep setting goals for yourself.

S	**SPECIFIC** What exactly do you want to accomplish?
M	**MEASURABLE** How will you know you have achieved your goal?
A	**ACTION** What steps will you take to achieve your goal?
R	**REALISTIC** Can you actually achieve this goal?
T	**TIME** What is the deadline to achieve this goal?
E	**EVALUATE** What steps do you need to adjust to achieve your goal?
R	**REWARD** How will you reward yourself when you achieve your goal?

SMARTER goals can take you far along your athletic journey. But what happens when life derails your plans? If you can't meet a goal due to an injury or having to travel for several weeks, or anything else that turns up unexpectedly, simply readjust your goals. It's okay to change them up when you need to. Just be sure to revisit them daily, and go over them in-depth once a month.

Remember, there are no little goals. Everything means something and is a part of the larger goal and outcome. Any little advantage you can give yourself can turn into a huge advantage for you and your team.

Remember, there are no little goals. Everything means something and is a part of the larger goal and outcome.

From Dreams to Reality

By now you can probably see just how important it is to have clearly defined goals, particularly short-term goals that help you methodically move toward your bigger ambitions and dreams. Goals are a must-have for athletes. You can't swing at the ball unless you've got a bat. Likewise, you can play your best only when there's a clear goal to focus on. For example, a great goal most players have is to play every game one pitch at a time. Slowing down and focusing on what's happening at that moment will bring your athletic talents to the game. It's not always easy to accomplish without the help of a solid mental game in hand.

Goals are a must-have for athletes. You can't swing at the ball unless you've got a bat. Likewise, you can play your best only when there's a clear goal to focus on.

Goals help you understand where you are right now and where you want to go. They ignite motivation and desire, help you commit to being your best, and build self-confidence that sustains you during slumps and helps you move past them. You can track your performance to improve your game and keep you solidly focused on what matters most to you and working with those around you. Dream big, then break those dreams into manageable step-by-step processes that will make that dream come true.

Dream big, then break those dreams into manageable step-by-step processes that will make that dream come true.

A solid system of short- and long-term goals is needed to proceed through this book. Let's make them together. The following exercises are meant to get you thinking even more about goal-setting.

It's fun to dream big and then use our dreams to make goals. You're welcome to break your dreams and goals into two parts, one for your general life and one for sport. For these upcoming activities, let yourself go, relax, and imagine everything you've ever wanted to do and where you'd like to go.

Dreams

1. I've always wanted to_____

   _____

2. It would be fun to _____

   _____

3. This might seem crazy or far-fetched, but I want to

   _____

   _____

4. Someone told me that I had a talent for _____

   _____

   and I could see myself doing that.

Now, let's take these dreams and mold them into goals.

Long-Term Goals

1. By (put a date here)_____

   I will (state the dream)_____

   _____

   a. I will know that I've achieved this goal because _____

   _____

    b. Am I willing to accomplish this goal?

    _____

    _____

    c. What are the steps I'll need to take to achieve this goal?_____

    _____

    _____

    d. What can I do tomorrow to achieve this goal?_____

    _____

2. By (put a date here) _____
I will (state the dream and keep going with more)

_____

    a. I will know that I've achieved this goal when

    _____

    b. Am I willing to accomplish this goal?

    _____

    _____

    c. What are the steps I'll need to take to achieve this goal? _____

    _____

    d. What can I do tomorrow to achieve this goal? _____

    _____

    _____

Short-Term Goals (Next, look at one of your long-term goals and start breaking it down into smaller steps.)

1. By (put a date here) _____

   I will _____

   _____

      a. I will know that I've achieved this goal

         because _____

         _____

      b. Am I willing to accomplish this goal?

         _____

         _____

      c. What are the steps I'll need to take to achieve

         this goal? _____

         _____

      d. What can I do tomorrow to achieve this

         goal? _____

         _____

2. By (put a date here) _____

   I will _____

   _____

      a. I will know that I've achieved this goal

         because _____

         _____

b. Am I willing to accomplish this goal?

_____

_____

c. What are the steps I'll need to take to achieve this goal? _____

_____

d. What can I do tomorrow to achieve this goal? _____

_____

3. By (put a date here)_____ I will

_____

a. I will know that I've achieved this goal because _____

_____

b. Am I willing to accomplish this goal?

_____

_____

c. What are the steps I'll need to take to achieve this goal? _____

_____

_____

d. What can I do tomorrow to achieve this goal?_____

_____

_____

4. By (put a date here)_____

I will _____

_____

    a. I will know that I've achieved this goal because _____

         _____

    b. Am I willing to accomplish this goal?

         _____

    c. What are the steps I'll need to take to achieve this goal? _____

         _____

    d. What can I do tomorrow to achieve this goal?_____

         _____

Here's a quick example of how this exercise may look:

1. Dream: I want to run a marathon.

2. Long-term goal: By (next May), I will run in a local marathon.
   a. I will know that I've achieved this goal because I will have run through the finish line (not walked), and I'll have a runner's number I can post on my bedroom wall as a trophy of my accomplishment.

b. Am I willing to accomplish this goal? Yes, especially since my friend has already run a marathon, and I want to beat his time.

c. What are the steps I'll need to take to achieve this goal? I need a training schedule and the motivation to train daily and eat the right foods.

d. What can I do tomorrow to achieve this goal? Go buy some running shoes and take my first run according to the training schedule.

3. Short-term goals to achieve this long-term goal: Stick to the training schedule for six months.

a. I will know that I've achieved this goal because I will keep a calendar and mark off how much I run and my time every day.

b. Am I willing to accomplish this goal? Yes, I don't want to be caught walking or risk getting injured during the race.

c. What are the steps I'll need to take to achieve this goal? I need to find a way to fit it into my work schedule. I need to ask for support from my friends/family. I need to be ready to sacrifice fun activities in order to stick to my schedule.

d. What can I do tomorrow to achieve this goal? I will start drinking more water, go grocery shopping for new food, and take a run according to the schedule.

Now What?

By now, you've got a plan (or at least the seeds of a plan) in place for reaching one or more long-term goals. There are a few more things you can do to ensure you stay inspired and stick to the outline you have created in this chapter.

First, go ahead and get your calendar out and start plugging in what you need to do every day in order to accomplish all of your goals. This can take time, but digital calendars make it easy because you can set recurring events and activities. And with digital calendars, you'll get a message when it's time to engage in your activity to reach your goal. Remember to put your larger goals down on your calendar as well. For example, on May 8, you will run your marathon.

This next step is very important for staying motivated to stick to your goals. Copy down your long-term goals onto a blank sheet of paper (make copies) and put them in places where you'll see them every day. Place them on your bathroom mirror, inside the door of your house so you can read it before you leave every day, on the refrigerator, in the car, and even in your locker.

Copy down your long-term goals onto a blank sheet of paper (make copies) and put them in places where you'll see them every day.

This next step is also critical: Connect with two trusted people and share your goals with them. They will help hold you accountable. Make sure you choose people who will give you that little push you need to stick with it, and who will even ask you where you are in accomplishing your goals every once in a while.

Connect with two trusted people and share your goals with them. They will help hold you accountable.

Coach Tip:

If you haven't already done so, create your own goals and go through this process yourself. Maybe share some of the goals with your players and show them how you are working toward accomplishing them for yourself and for them. Check in with your athletes at least once a week and ask them to share their goals and how they are doing with them. When everyone is doing it, then there's even more accountability to sticking with it, and you'll see motivation rising and positive energy flowing.

Parent Tip:

Why not join your athlete on this important journey and make your own goals? Share at least one long-term goal and the short-term goals that lead to accomplishing your dream with your athlete, then live it daily as an example of what it takes and what it looks like to work for your dreams and accomplish goals. Doing this adds more buy-in from your athlete who sees the rewards of sticking it out to meet goals and the personal satisfaction that comes with it. Give it a go! There's nothing to lose and everything great to gain.

Chapter Work-Up: Points to Remember as You Set Goals

Come back to this chapter tomorrow and review your goals. Put an alert on your calendar and make time to sit down and go over them with the following points in mind so you can add more to your goals, add new goals, or change them.

1. Make them positive. State what you will do, not what you don't want to do or won't do. Focus on what you can achieve, not what you want to avoid.

2. Prioritize your goals. Doing this eliminates the feeling of being overwhelmed that leads to giving up before you begin. Direct your attention to what goals mean the most for you right now in your life. Making the baseball team is more important than running the marathon if you're not interested in a career as a marathon runner.

3. Identify the barriers to reaching your goals. What are they and how will you overcome them? Injuries, moving out of your area, or challenges in

your home or personal life can put up roadblocks, but with some creative thinking, problem-solving, and rearranging your goals, you can stay on track. And remember, your own negative mindset can also be a barrier; your first line of defense is always a positive attitude.

4. Emphasize the process, not the outcome. Make sure you have control over your goals and are focusing on achieving individual skills or behaviors instead of emphasizing the outcome. For example, you want to run that marathon and a new goal crops up after you see that you could possibly rank in the top 10 according to your running time. Instead of focusing on ranking in the top 10, stay laser-focused on your goal of building endurance. Make sure not to run too fast in the first five miles and learn to talk to yourself about balancing your pace while you do practice runs.

5. Review your goals often. Read through them entirely and see if any modifications are needed or if priorities need to be switched. Right now, get out your calendar and pick a date every month to review your goals.

6. Enjoy your success. When you achieve a short-term or long-term goal, go ahead and celebrate it. Share it with friends and family and

know that you've filled up your self-confidence bank account.

When you achieve a short-term or long-term goal, go ahead and celebrate it. Share it with friends and family and know that you've filled up your self-confidence bank account.

PERFORMANCE JOURNAL

CHAPTER SIX

Work Ethic

"Failure to prepare is preparing to fail."
—Every good coach

Your work ethic impacts every aspect of your role as an athlete and as a human being. It impacts your attitude and what you do daily, including how you show up to practice, how much you push yourself during conditioning and strength training, how you get along with your coach and teammates, and so much more.

Work ethic encompasses traits such as honesty, integrity, humility, dedication, responsibility, preparation, and accountability. These traits dictate how you act toward others or how you react to negative situations. Do you slam the door when you're mad, or do you take deep breaths and go for a walk? Do you tell the coach you were late for the second time this week because of bad traffic when really you were trying to finish up messaging your friend, or do you apologize and work to be on time tomorrow?

Your identity, your personality, who you are, is all linked to your work ethic. A strong work ethic is all about treating others well, putting in extra effort when it is not asked of you, being humble, playing to help your team win (not just to get cheers from the crowd), and being honest not only to others but to yourself. Anything less is a shoddy work ethic that will get you nowhere.

> **Your identity, your personality, who you are, is all linked to your work ethic.**

To be a champion, you must hone your work ethic, and that takes daily effort that encompasses your conditioning, your thoughts, and your actions. I regularly tell my players, "If you are not practicing, somebody else is, somewhere, and they will be ready to take your position." And of course, your work ethic affects the way you play and the game as a whole. The bottom line: Get your work ethic straight, and nothing will stop you from being the best.

> **I regularly tell my players, "If you are not practicing, somebody else is, somewhere, and they will be ready to take your position."**

Putting the Six Ps into Practice

There's a popular adage from the British Army that goes "Proper Planning and Preparation Prevents Piss-Poor Performance." I have adapted it to further draw your attention to the effectiveness of a strong work ethic. I call it the Six Ps of Work Ethic: Proper Psychological Practice Prevents Poor Performance. If you take this to heart and work on your mindset daily, in addition to putting in long hours of practicing the athletic fundamentals of your sport, you will perform like a champion, because nothing—including the mental side of your performance—will hold you back. Here's what it can look like:

It's mid-season, and the team is experiencing a lull. They are still working hard, but their minds have become complacent, and the excitement of pre-season is long gone. You've caught yourself caring less too—you even missed weight training this week and didn't admit to it. Your work ethic is all but gone. In its place is dishonesty, laziness, and pride, and your head is totally out of the game. It's not fair for you, and definitely not fair to your coach and team. It's time to get back on track.

First, do a head check.

This questionnaire helps you find out where your work ethic stands. As always, be truthful with your responses; if you're not honest, you won't improve. Nor will you get the most out of this book. We're here to become champions, so let's move forward.

1. The coach asks you to do 30 push-ups every morning as soon as your feet hit the floor. You . . .
   a. Do exactly 30.
   b. Do a couple more each time; sometimes you do 32, and other days it's 40.
   c. Do the push-ups at school or basically in front of someone. It helps motivate you.
   d. Do the push-ups first thing in the morning while focusing on what you want to accomplish this year: get stronger, run faster, stay healthy, be on time.

Read all of the below options as they pertain to everyone. Life circumstances can land you in a different place, turning your once-insatiable appetite for being the best to indifference. If you chose...

a. You have an **Average Work Ethic**: This means you do enough to get by with what's asked of you and no more. This is fine, and it works for a while, but when the tough times come, you won't know how to overcome them. Don't worry; you can easily work your way up by challenging yourself (goal-setting, self-talk) to do more. Do more push-ups and write your goals down and post them up on your wall and in your car.

b. You have a **Strong Work Ethic**: You've got the fundamentals of working hard down; now it's time to really push to study and implement the mental techniques in this book. If you're doing extra physical exercise such as laps and push-ups, work on a gratitude list at the same time. Your body and mind can work at the same time. You can do the extra work on your own time, and that's great, but remember to use your mental training techniques during practice, too.

c. You have a **Pretend Work Ethic**: It's not as bad as you think, and that's the point. You like accolades and looking good when people are watching, and that's okay, but you need to ask yourself the question: *Why am I doing this? Do I love the act of gaining muscle and discipline so I can be an elite athlete and make myself and coach proud, or do I just like this because it's the sport* *that gives me the best chance at fame?* If you're looking for the spotlight, you'll miss the ball—it will literally go right past you while you're blinded by the flashing lights. Challenge yourself to work hard in order to be great for others. Young athletes are often encouraged to have a fake-it-until-you-make-it attitude because it works. But now it's time to step up from that and really dig in.

If you're looking for the spotlight, you'll miss the ball—it will literally go right past you while you're blinded by the flashing lights. Challenge yourself to work hard in order to be great for others.

d. You have an **Exceptional Work Ethic**: Here's the good news: Having an exceptional work ethic is contagious. You naturally draw people in and inspire them to work harder themselves. This may sound like you're the best thing since sliced bread, but really, you're in danger of hitting a wall—either from picking up others' slack, or dealing with life circumstances or even an injury that seems insurmountable. Like the saying goes: The taller they are, the harder they fall. Chapters 9 and 10 are very important for you. Because of your exceptional work ethic, you may already be working on the mental part of your game. Make sure to work daily on mental training and focus exercises, remembering they are just as important, if not more so, than the physical. You might trend toward being impatient or even angry with others who don't work as hard as you do. But try to be patient, and ask them questions about the issues they're facing to get perspective and inspire them to stick with their commitments.

The Keys to a Strong Work Ethic

There are three key components that you can focus on to strengthen your work ethic: preparation, dedication, and responsibility. We will take a closer look at each of these building blocks in the next section.

There are three key components that you can focus on to strengthen your work ethic: preparation, dedication, and responsibility.

Preparation is the action and repetition of learning. In order to build real confidence (the kind that doesn't disappear when you face an insurmountable challenge), you must practice until you can complete the task with ease. But practicing a task over and over again until you can repeat it without limitations requires a number of mental elements: positivity, goal-setting, mental toughness, and resilience. In short, your body will take you only so far. It will say it's tired, but if your goal was to do twice as much today, your mind is already prepared to imagine how good it will feel to do more and prove that you can reach your goal. That's the recipe for a champion.

Dedication is another key component of work ethic. When you have a desire to be the best, have goals to make this desire real, and add dedication, you get success. The more you commit to devoting energy to both your physical and mental exercises and efforts, the more your work ethic will increase. With dedication, you'll notice a natural instinct to work out harder, watch more videos of your favorite players or competition, and care more about working on your goals every day.

My advice to young players is to make a decision to want to get better. Say it out loud and write it on your wall: *I am going to do what it takes to be better. I'm going to work hard and practice every day.* To make this a reality, be the best you can be at every moment. Take the time to practice what you need to practice. Focus on it; give every aspect your full attention.

> **Say it out loud and write it on your wall:** I am going to do what it takes to be better. I'm going to work hard and practice every day.

Hall of Famer Don Mattingly said to ESPN/MLB Network reporter Peter Gammons, "I want to improve every day in every facet of the game. I hate to hear that a guy's not a good defensive player. There shouldn't be any bad defensive players, not if they work hard enough. It's as simple as that. There are tons of players who could be a lot better. I'd like to have some of the talents of those guys. Give me their talent, and I'll do some really big things."

Ironically, former Yankees great Mickey Mantle was looking back on the ratio between talent and dedication during his playing days. He claimed to regret the years that he felt he "took off" during his career that kept him from reaching some of his goals. He stated that kids with love for the game owe it to themselves and the game to do everything they can to get better and go as far as they can go in the game of baseball.

The bottom line here is: Dedicate yourself entirely to your sport. You will amaze yourself with the results.

Dedicate yourself entirely to your sport. You will amaze yourself with the results.

Responsibility is the next major key to an exceptional work ethic. You cannot control what happens to you, but you can control your reaction to whatever happens. Take responsibility for how you respond to both negative and positive outcomes that are out of your control.

You cannot control what happens to you, but you can control your reaction to whatever happens.

Think about this scenario: You're up to bat with two strikes, the bases are loaded, and your team is behind several runs. Then the umpire calls the third strike when the ball was obviously out of the box. This was your big chance! The ump is blind! You're furious. You know you can't change the call by throwing a fit, so now is the time to take responsibility for the first two strikes. Review what happened, come up with some solutions, and do better next time by slowing things down in your favor.

Here are some tips to help you build responsibility.

1. Have a clearly defined mission while you're playing and practicing. "I'm going to be patient and not swing too soon."

2. Play the game one pitch at a time. "I'm going to be in control of myself. I have a plan and purpose for each pitch. I'm going to trust myself."

3. Focus on the process, not the outcome. Pay attention entirely to the process of playing the game and forget individual results. For example, focus on the process of fielding a ground ball. If you missed it, don't focus on the miss; focus on how you missed it.

4. Develop your mental skills (you're already doing that by reading this book). Learn about mental

imagery. Imagine what you look like and feel like getting that ground ball. Try throwing in some positive self-talk about how you're focusing on the next play, not the last.

5. Make a commitment to learn daily. Get in the habit of evaluating each of your performances, breaking them down to see where you can do better.

Work-Ethic Boosters & Suckers

Here's the deal: Downtime with friends is a must, but downtime with people who are constantly in downtime-mode will eat at your work ethic. It can be difficult, but sometimes you need to spend more time working on you and less time hanging out with friends who don't work at much of anything. It's not about dumping these friends; it's about prioritizing your time with them.

> *Downtime with friends is a must,*
> *but downtime with people who are*
> *constantly in downtime-mode will*
> *eat at your work ethic.*

The first step is identifying those people who are work-ethic boosters and those who are work-ethic suckers. Next, we'll go over how to get your schedule filled mostly with work-ethic boosters while still making a little time for the work-ethic suckers.

Think about one of your friends whom you hang out with regularly. Answer these questions with that one person in mind. Then do it again with the next buddy. You can also include your family members. Put them in either category and keep them there.

1. When you're with your friend, do you go out and do something physically active, or do you sit on the couch and play video games?

2. Does your buddy ask you for a lot of favors? If their idea of a good time is hitting the couch and

asking *you* to go buy the snacks, you've got to put them in the Work-Ethic Sucker category.

3. Does your friend (or family member) show up to your games? If they show up to at least two or three games a season, put them in the Work-Ethic Booster category. Otherwise, relegate them to the Work-Ethic Suckers pile.

4. Do they support your efforts to spend extra time working out to become a better athlete and person? If so, they belong in the Work-Ethic Booster category.

5. Do you have to call your friend (or family member) and ask them to hang out, or do they call you? If you have to do most of the calling, put them in the Work-Ethic Suckers Category.

6. When you do go hang with a friend, do they usually have the plans set, or do you? If you both equally come up with the plan, then set them in the Work-Ethic Booster category.

Use the blank space on the next page to write down the two categories. Label column one "Work-Ethic Boosters," and label the second column "Work-Ethic Suckers." Fill in the spaces with the names of the people in your life, even the group you have lunch with every day. If they can be both, write their name right down the middle.

_____   _____

_____   _____

_____   _____

_____   _____

_____   _____

_____   _____

_____   _____

Now it's time to prioritize. Give each person in the Booster column priority time over the people in the Sucker column. You should hang out with those in the Sucker category less frequently, and hang out with them more during the offseason when you can truly let loose. But when you're in-season, and training is paramount, you must surround yourself with upbeat, energetic people who add to your positive energy. When you are dog-tired from running drills, they'll be okay hanging on the couch playing video games, but they will also ask you how you're doing and actually listen. And they'll get you excited about tomorrow and tackling your rigorous schedule because they know it matters to you.

When you're in-season, and training is paramount, you must surround yourself with upbeat, energetic people who add to your positive energy.

The Work-Ethic Suckers may do the opposite. You probably won't find them at the park playing pick-up basketball. If someone on your Work-Ethic Suckers list happens to be an athlete, they will likely complain a lot about their schedule or how bad this player or that coach is and not offer any solutions. Give these guys a more limited amount of your time. Our lifelong friends can mean a lot to us, and that's okay. But make sure you don't let their attitude and lack of work ethic affect you.

You may ask: *What if family members I live with turn out to be work-ethic suckers?* It can be tough if your brother is a drag or if your parents don't appreciate how much work it is to juggle what you do. The key is to create your environment and put boundaries up to protect it.

The key is to create your environment and put boundaries up to protect it.

It's both a physical construct and a mental one. For the physical aspect, set up your bedroom so you can focus and shut out the world. Put up motivational posters—even an image of a racecar speeding through the desert works. Fill your room with items that help you get your work done, such as a wall clock, weights, and a mini-fridge full of

Gatorade and cheese snacks. Add some plants to clean up the air and make it feel livable.

After you've created the space, protect it in the same way you protect your thoughts. Don't allow people to come into your room and trash it with their empty drink bottles and wrappers. Certainly don't allow anyone to smoke dope or vape either, because that's counter to keeping your body at its best. If you don't feel you can stand up to your buddy about their disruptive habits, then change your feeling. Feel upset that they don't respect you and how hard you are working to achieve big goals. You are no good to your team or yourself if you can't stand up to your friends and be truthful. Put your hand up, tell them clearly what is not welcome in your space, and then move on to something productive.

> **You are no good to your team or yourself if you can't stand up to your friends and be truthful. Put your hand up, tell them clearly what is not welcome in your space, and then move on to something productive.**

The same goes for disallowing some of your own negative thoughts, for they too can become Work-Ethic Suckers. When you have thoughts about not being good enough, making too many errors, or even making the worst mistake ever, stand guard at the door of your room and tell them, *You're not welcome here.* The most critical next step is to move on with a better thought—for example, *I'll do some push-ups instead.* Drop and do at least 40, telling yourself the entire time, *This is making me better. I want to be better.* Tell yourself what you want. Stand guard at your door and protect your space.

> **When you have thoughts about not being good enough, making too many errors, or even making the worst mistake ever, stand guard at the door of your room and tell them, You're not welcome here.**

Stick to these practices, and soon you will build yourself a space to create a work ethic worthy of a great athlete.

Coach Tip:

In my coaching experience, I've seen many coaches give up on athletes who lose the desire to play and may not have come onto the team with much of a desire in the first place. Many of these athletes need only a good one-on-one conversation, asking them some of the very questions put forth in this book.

Start by asking them why they are there. What do they like? What gets them fired up? What are their goals? If they don't have any goals right now, take a minute and help create a couple of simple and achievable goals with them.

Based on how you've watched them play, you can also help them come up with a motivating phrase, and get

them excited about using it when they are feeling unin-
spired. Ask them every day when you see them to tell you
the phrase and repeat it back to them. Your attention alone
will create a desire in them and a sense of loyalty to you and
the team. I've seen this approach work time and again.
Average players rise to become great athletes, so don't give
up on them.

*Average players rise to become great
athletes, so don't give up on them.*

Parent Tip:

Because you live with your athlete, it really helps to
engage them by giving them housework and yard work and
speak to them about how this chapter on work ethic relates
to everyday tasks and responsibilities.

For example, even on days when it's not their job or
responsibility to take out the garbage, emphasize to your
athlete that they can still do it simply because they have a
moment. Point out that it makes people feel good to contribute and that this selfless contribution helps others.

Your goal should be to help your athlete practice and
understand what it means to go above and beyond and to
create experiences that build their work ethic. As you probably know, young adults and children generally don't want
to be told what to do or have someone hover over them;
sometimes this even results in them doing less work. If this
is the case with your athlete, show; don't tell. When you see

something that needs to be done, or someone who needs help, step in and lend a hand without having to be asked. This sets a powerful example that they will remember. Also, show them what it looks like to do the work without looking for accolades or validation from someone else. The reward is the good feelings you receive by doing something nice and the invaluable self-worth this creates.

Your goal should be to help your athlete practice and understand what it means to go above and beyond and to create experiences that build their work ethic.

Chapter Work-Up:

"Your mind is the toughest opponent you must face and defeat to be successful in sports and in life."

—David Angeron

It's time for a little self-evaluation to see where your work ethic stands now, and give you an idea of where you could use improvement. Answer these questions below, designed specifically to evaluate work ethic:

1. Can you describe a time when you went the extra mile at practice?

2. When things are slow or you've finished your tasks, what do you do?

3. How do you define work ethic? What does it mean to you?

4. When have you worked the hardest? Describe the situation and explain your motivation.

5. Give an example of when you completed a difficult task that made you work harder than normal.

Hopefully by now you're feeling ready to work hard to be the best athlete you can be. Here is some great advice that I refer to often when I want to feel inspired and motivated to do my best work. These tips come from Brian Cain, a world-renowned mental performance coach and the creator of the Mental Performance Mastery (MPM) Coaches Certification Course and 30 Days to MPM for Athletes Program (BrianCain.com). Keep these insights and directives in mind as you continue strengthening your work ethic. They will energize you and get you back on track whenever you feel like slacking off or giving up.

Force Yourself to Act Different from How You Feel

There will be days that you are not motivated, don't feel good, are in a bad mood, or don't feel confident. On these days, you need to learn to pretend. Learn to become an actor. If you are in a bad mood, pretend you're in a good mood and get your work done. If you don't feel confident, pretend you are feeling confident and get your work done.

Champions Are Not Born; They Are Made

Very few people are truly committed to the pursuit of excellence. Get used to looking at yourself in the mirror and answering to yourself, because every night, when that head hits the pillow, that's the person you're going to answer to. Other people are going to tell you you can't do it. That you're not big enough, fast enough, or strong enough. Or even worse, you may be surrounded by a bunch of yes-people who tell you that you're the best when you are really quite average. You just can't listen, because champions know it doesn't matter what people think, because champions are made—they're developed—they're not born, and *anyone* can be a champion if they are committed to excellence and follow the fundamentals.

Motivation Is a Daily Decision

To stay motivated, you've got to surround yourself with things that motivate you. Do you have a vision board posted in your office, room, car, or locker that shows you what you want to accomplish? Consider this advertising to yourself. Coke and Pepsi are the two most famous soft drinks, and that is largely due to the fact that they saturate the market and your head with advertising. You want to advertise to yourself on a daily basis with vision boards, photos of your next opponent, quotes or goals written on your bathroom mirror with a dry erase marker, and by reading a lot from good books.

Stop Counting Down the Days and Start Making Those Days Count

Champions also know that you don't count the days 'til the next fight, but make the days count. They set long-term goals of where they want to be at the end of the year, but commit 100 percent to that day's goal, to the here and now. They realize that yesterday is history, tomorrow is a mystery, and today is a gift—that's why we call it the present. They live for today and get the most out of today, because they know their career and life will be the sum of all their todays.

What's Important Now

Right now, today. What are you going to do today to get better? What is your goal for today? Do you see a pattern developing here? Throughout each day, there are going to be distractions, fish hooks that rip you out of the water while you are searching for your goals. When you get side-tracked, get off at the wrong exit on your way to work, realize that you must get back in the moment—that winning is an end result that takes care of itself if you win the moment. You win the moment by remembering What's Important Now!

You win the moment by remembering What's Important Now!

This is the last chapter of the first section of this book. This section has been dedicated to helping you find out who you are while creating a solid foundation upon which to build your Mental Master Method. From here, you will learn all the techniques used by elite athletes who have tested them and proven that they lead to greatness on and off the field.

Get ready to walk among the greatest athletes in the world and build your mental muscle. Soon you will be ready to walk out onto the field with confidence and watch the game slow down so you have time to make game-changing, split-second decisions. In short, you're about to learn the secrets that will free you to enjoy your sport to the fullest extent possible.

PERFORMANCE JOURNAL

CHAPTER SEVEN

Confidence

"If you have confidence, you will perform at the level you aspire to. If you have fear, you will never achieve that level. "
—Augie Garrido

Every year, about midway through the season, I call a special team meeting. I always make sure it's not too early in the season because I don't want the players to peak too soon. Doing it at the halfway point gives them enough time to evaluate themselves and their teammates.

The topic of this special meeting is confidence. I always start out by getting each athlete to evaluate themselves. They let me know how they feel they have been playing, what they have been doing well, and what they could be doing better. Then I ask the entire group who they believe is the best player on the team.

Each year, the team inevitably looks around the room for a bit, and finally, one person mentions a name. For example, they might say so-and-so is the best player because he throws the hardest. Before long someone offers up another name because that guy is the fastest, or another because he's the smoothest defender. After several minutes of discussion about who's the best player on the team, I tell them they all have the wrong answer.

The Correct Answer Is, "I Am."

When I ask my teams who the best player on the team is, the only answer I ever want to hear out of everyone's mouth is, "I AM." Why? Because I want each of my players to believe in themselves. I don't want to make them cocky or convince them that they are better than everyone else. I simply want them to build confidence in themselves, because when players believe in themselves, they play better. This causes a positive ripple effect that impacts the whole team. When one person plays better, the teammate next to them plays better. And if each member of the team is playing as if they are the best player on the team, then the other members not only believe in themselves, they also believe in the other guys around them. The confidence is contagious, and a recipe for success.

If each member of the team is playing as if they are the best player on the team, then the other members not only believe in themselves, they also believe in the other guys around them. The confidence is contagious, and a recipe for success.

Building life skills through sport is something I am passionate about, and one of the fundamentally important life skills that translates the most effectively is self-confidence. You can take the confidence you gain in your sport off the field and use it in all areas of your life. Self-confidence not only helps you become a great athlete, it helps you do better in your school work, it helps you build strong relationships with your parents and peers, and it transforms you into a true leader on and off the field. True confidence helps you become a more balanced human being overall.

True confidence helps you become a more balanced human being overall.

This chapter is the starting point where you begin creating your Mental Master Method. Everything you have learned up to this point has prepared you for this moment. You now know yourself better; you know who you are, why you play your sport(s), what your attitude is as an athlete, and which goals you want to pursue moving forward. Starting now, you will learn about mental mastery and creating your own Mental Master Method using the techniques and elements you will pick up through the rest of this book.

As you read the following chapters, I want you to remember that you are not your batting average. But you *are* how you react to and think about your batting average. What you do with that information is what enables you to make your Mental Master Method. It is not focused on extra hours in the pen; instead it is about taking a moment every day to prepare for practice mentally. It's about being present during every pitch and consistently reviewing your performance. Keep completing the chapter work-ups, because in the last chapter, you'll compile all your notes and answers to create your Mental Master Method.

I want you to remember that you are not your batting average. But you are how you react to and think about your batting average.

This chapter is invaluable for every player, including you. At some point in your sport career, you will face adversity that will have you questioning your ability and wondering why you're still playing. But creating a solid platform built on real confidence will give you a bridge you can use to walk over those fires.

Do You Have Confidence When It Counts?

Here is the most important fact I want you to remember about confidence: It is based on your beliefs and your inner self. It is not based on external factors like other people's opinions of you, your most recent athletic performance (regardless of whether that performance was good or not-so-good), or the numbers you're trying to reach.

When confidence is based on praise from others, or from winning an award, or from beating a number, it is not genuine and it will not be there when it counts. Real confidence, the kind that remains no matter the failure, is built by honest striving, constant pushing through difficulties, and using your inner resources to rebound and come back stronger.

Real confidence, the kind that remains no matter the failure, is built by honest striving, constant pushing through difficulties, and using your inner resources to rebound and come back stronger.

Other people cannot give you true confidence—not your coach, not your girlfriend, not your buddies, and not your parents. What may feel like confidence based on others' approval or praise is a false sense of confidence, also known as pride.

So, how do you know if you're truly confident or not? The answer is simple. Look for doubt and uncertainty. These feelings are the opposite of confidence. If you doubt whether or not you can do something, then you already have your answer: You can't. If you're uncertain about the way you'll respond to a given situation, then you lack confidence. Check in with yourself before games and ask yourself if you're truly certain you can handle the pressure of fulfilling your role at first base in the bottom of the ninth while playing a team that's beaten you before. Can you overcome your weakness and make the play when it counts?

So, how do you know if you're truly confident or not? The answer is simple. Look for doubt and uncertainty.

It's okay to admit it if right now the answer is "no." It's best to work through this by building your confidence to the point where you can play your sport with a mindset that nothing will stand in the way of what you want to achieve.

Your ultimate goal is to have a strong mental game, and that takes a foundation of confidence. I am not implying that confident people with strong mental games always win, but they fare better than people who lack confidence. Without confidence, everything you do requires more work, and you'll find mistakes and negative emotions looping back to you over and over again.

Your ultimate goal is to have a strong mental game, and that takes a foundation of confidence.

Baseball, in particular, is a mentally difficult game, because every player faces a lot of adversity and failure. You can easily lose control of your performance and wind up in a slump that's difficult to escape if you don't tackle it quickly. To regain control, you must tap into your confidence. You can be the confident player who recognizes where improvement is needed and quickly begins focusing on the strong positive thoughts and images that help you move toward those improvements. Then your thoughts about yourself will be filled with images of you making great plays, enjoying the game, and telling yourself, *Nothing gets by me.*

Confidence is easy to spot. Confident people move smoothly and have a presence of calm control. They are usually free of fear, doubt, and stress. They are poised for action, ready to sharpen their focus one minute and break into a celebratory smile the next. Meanwhile, players who lack confidence often show their anger, anxiety, or fear by slouching, throwing gear, swearing, or hesitating at crucial moments. Each of these behaviors and the emotions that cause them are obstacles to good performance. They show the player is not in control and certainly not confident. Remember, it's your thinking that determines whether you are in control or not. It's up to you to create confidence that will eliminate the negative emotional obstacles that get in the way of your best performances.

Remember, it's your thinking that determines whether you are in control or not. It's up to you to create confidence that will eliminate the negative emotional obstacles that get in the way of your best performances.

Building confidence should be a priority for any elite athlete. Try the following tips to develop true confidence that will help you perform your best.

First, decide that you will never stop. This is the first and most crucial step: Never stop striving to be the best and meet your goals. Never stop trying to win. Want to gain more muscle? Stand up right now, take a step forward, then another, and turn those into lunges. There's always an opportunity for improvement. It is a choice to make something out of nothing, and the only way to do this is to keep going. That leads to self-satisfaction, which leads to confidence and a mindset that you can't be stopped.

Adopt a "never lose" philosophy. Yes, you will still lose at times, but with a "never lose" philosophy, you will feel and focus on those losses for only the briefest moment. Then you will start contemplating how you can do better next time. Before you know it, you're immediately back to striving, hungry for the next challenge that always is leading to the next win.

Always look forward. There's only one direction: forward. Moving and thinking about what's next, and how you're going to tackle it, is all that matters. Always looking for the next win is a surefire way to build your confidence, because your mind is always focused on doing what it takes to overcome challenges or losses and get better.

Allow zero procrastination. Whenever you think of doing something that will bring you closer to your goals, do it immediately. Making long lists is just another way of procrastinating. Sure, it's necessary to make lists when there's a lot to do, and you can't do everything at midnight, but generally speaking, do it the moment you think of it. If you can't possibly do it until tomorrow, write it down on your list of what's happening tomorrow. Prioritize it compared to what else is on your list; you don't get to think about anything else on your list until the first—the most important one—is done.

Stay in constant motion. This initiative ties in closely with never stopping. Constantly take action that drives you forward. The simple act of doing something as soon as you think about it not only saves time but keeps you moving forward without having to plan it. What's the point in planning to go work out at the gym when you skipped today's workout? Take yourself to the gym today, or if it's closed, take a run instead. Now you no longer have to put it on the calendar and worry that it will crowd your schedule tomorrow.

Coach Tip:

Coaches, when facing problems with an athlete's performance, resolve to consider and investigate the mental side and not just the technical or physical side. Technique is not always the answer to an athlete's issues. Is technique going to help them when they struggle with a lack of confidence every time they're faced with adversity? No. Technique is only as good as the mind behind it. And if the mind behind the technique is on shaky ground, technique loses every time. Even professional athletes falter due to their own thoughts, because the mental part of the game rules supreme.

Technique is only as good as the mind behind it. And if the mind behind the technique is on shaky ground, technique loses every time.

Here are some solutions. Ask the athlete a series of questions to help them think about how their mental game might be interfering with their performance. Be sure to ask each athlete these questions privately and to always speak to them in a calm manner.

Ask, "How did it feel when..." questions, and then inquire as to how they would solve the issue themselves. They may not have a ready answer, and that's okay. Next, ask them to spend time thinking about it, then follow-up with them the next day. When the athlete owns and implements the solution they come up with (even if you helped guide them to a more refined solution), their confidence will grow exponentially. Guide them through this process throughout the season.

Parent Tip:

As a parent, the mental and physical health of your athlete are paramount, while your opinion of their performance and what could have made it better may need to take the backseat for now. The best way to help your athlete to grow into an independent adult who can make confident decisions on their own is to ask them questions and listen. Let your questions guide them to solutions they can own. The more your athlete owns their ideas and works to implement them, the more confident and successful they will be.

As a parent, the mental and physical health of your athlete are paramount, while your opinion of their performance and what could have made it better may need to take the backseat for now.

Chapter Work-Up:

Confidence is built on you believing in yourself. It's easy to be confident when you know what to expect and how you'll perform, but even seasoned professionals falter under pressure or can't find their way out of ruts. So, needless to say, you will struggle with these issues too. When this happens, you need a clear way out of the rut—a hand to pull you up when you're hanging from the cliff. That helping hand is you. By investing in the elements taught in the next eight chapters, you'll learn to create your Mental Master Method. Start by answering the following:

1. When do you feel the most confident? (for example: when I'm at bat, as catcher, or when I'm playing a pick-up game at the park with friends)

_____

_____

_____

2. Picture a time in your life when you were confident. Take a moment and try to feel that feeling right now. What made it memorable? What did you like about it?

_____

_____

_____

3. Was part of the reason you felt confident in this moment because you were with your teammates, or was it just you?

_____

_____

_____

4. Do you get down on yourself when you don't hit your numbers?

_____

_____

_____

5. Does it bother you when someone besides your coach tells you how to make your performance better?

_____

_____

_____

Now that you've given the topic of confidence some thought, it's time to create a confidence phrase that you'll take everywhere (it will help you through tests, hard conversations, through losses, and to first base). Do you have a favorite quote? A favorite spiritual verse? A word or phrase that encompasses energy and excitement? Write down what comes to your mind. Don't edit it; just get it down on paper.

_____

_____

_____

Next, take what you have written and form one short and meaningful phrase. (When you speak it, you should be able to feel the message in your bones, and feel it changing you for the better.) Here are some examples. Some of them may seem silly, but they are personal and speak to a person's experiences.

- "There it went; now here I come."
- "I can rest tomorrow. Only this matters right now."
- "Hooya, heck yeah!"
- "I'm confident. I'm positive. I'm doing this for the team."

Go ahead and write down several options, and if you haven't yet found the one you like the most, keep searching for it. Every day, add to the list until it hits you. A phrase or word will come, maybe after something significant happens to you, and that will be it. Use a temporary phrase until the perfect one shows up. Write it down in big, bold letters and post it up everywhere. Put it next to your goals and memorize it. Then start using it by repeating it to yourself during practices and games.

Now that you're well on your way to building your confidence, be sure to keep practicing the tools you were taught in this chapter. Confidence is crucial to your future as an athlete. If you don't tackle it now, you will eventually end up back here, because confidence is like a pair of cleats: You need it to play.

Confidence is like a pair of cleats: You need it to play.

PERFORMANCE JOURNAL

CHAPTER EIGHT

Positive Energy

"If you have positive energy, you will attract positive outcomes."
—Steve Backley

A few years ago, I was asked to coach baseball at a high school in South Louisiana. At the time, I had no plans for getting back into coaching; however, I viewed it as a challenge and looked forward to helping a program in need. Also, the person who called me about the position was a friend who happened to coach basketball at the same school. I quickly became excited about this unexpected opportunity.

The school was full of athletes, but many of them focused on football and basketball, so their baseball program struggled. Furthermore, the school was in a rough area, the players came from tough backgrounds, and the program didn't get much support. I am always looking for ways to help other people, and this was just another opportunity for me to take a negative situation and turn it into something positive. I had made up my mind; I was going to turn around this baseball program.

> *I had made up my mind; I was going to turn around this baseball program.*

A Cinderella Story in the Making

It was definitely a challenging season. I spent 95 percent of the year training and developing the athletes' mental approach to the game. Unfortunately, the team allowed outside circumstances to affect them mentally—either a bad call by the umpire, or one of the opposing player's trash-talking, or the fans' comments would badly rattle and derail us. We frequently lost focus and struggled to get over that mental hump.

Halfway through the season, I asked the players to sign a contract promising to put forth maximum effort, to play with a positive attitude, and to not let adversity or outside noise break their spirit and focus. Things didn't suddenly improve, but I could immediately see that the players had bought into a team concept. They had become mentally stronger. They just needed to put that collective strength into all three phases of the game—pitching, hitting, and defense. Nine seniors also realized their season would come to an end soon if they didn't act fast to turn things around.

They had become mentally stronger. They just needed to put that collective strength into all three phases of the game—pitching, hitting, and defense.

My assistant coach, whom we called Coach AD, was a football coach who had never coached baseball before. Coach AD's biggest asset to the team was his positive energy. He was always cheering and pumping the players up, and that was the most effective motivational tactic that worked with our players. Anytime we needed a little spark of inspiration, Coach AD would yell, "Give me three claps and a Ric Flair!" The team would follow, clapping three times together and yelling, "Wooooo!" after the claps. For those of you who don't know who Ric Flair is, he is a former wrestler famous for getting in the ring and yelling, "Wooooo!" Coach AD always knew the right time to get the players fired up with this ritual.

Anytime we needed a little spark of inspiration, Coach AD would yell, "Give me three claps and a Ric Flair!" The team would follow, clapping three times together and yelling, "Wooooo!" after the claps.

By the end of the season, the team had made great strides mentally, and we squeaked into the playoffs as the number 31 seed of 32 possible playoff spots. All of our seniors had committed to the mental process I had taught them throughout the season, and they were all actively taking on positive leadership roles within the team. Well, all except for one. This one senior was a great athlete, but he really struggled with the mental side of the game. He always wanted to fight or talk trash to the other players and complained about umpires and other things.

During one of our playoff games, this player was our starting shortstop. Early in the game, he started complaining about the umpire. I told him to change his attitude and stay positive. By the fifth inning, we couldn't get a break and were down 4-0 when Coach AD did his thing and yelled, "Give me three claps and a Ric Flair!" The team all clapped three times followed by, "Wooooo!" except for my shortstop. I heard him on the end of the bench say, "Give me three claps and the umpire sucks."

I immediately kicked him out of the dugout and replaced him with a freshman. So there went my best shortstop in the middle of a playoff game, with us down by four late in the game. I knew this meant we probably wouldn't be able to make a comeback, but we had worked too hard on positive energy and mental toughness for me to allow a senior to be a negative influence on our younger players.

During the next couple of innings, things began to change. We started getting the breaks we weren't getting early in the game. We scored three runs in the sixth inning and two more in the bottom of the seventh to win 5-4 and advance to the next round of the playoffs. Lesson learned: Good things happen to positive people and positive teams.

Lesson learned: Good things happen to positive people and positive teams.

After the game, my shortstop realized the mistake he had made. While crying, he came up, hugged me, and even apologized. He realized his baseball career was almost over, and he was choosing to end it on a negative note, all over some calls by one umpire.

I cared for him just as much as I cared for all of my players and gave him a second chance to come back on the team, but only if he vowed to stay positive the rest of the season. He became a totally different player that day. He ended up being one of the most exciting playmakers and positive leaders for us through the remainder of the playoffs and was a huge part of how we became the Cinderella story of the lowest-seeded team ever to reach the State Tournament in Louisiana history. You can see more about our Cinderella run and the mental toughness we built at https://www.mentalmastertraining.com/articles.

Even though I know that mental training is key to peak performance and have seen it work time and again, it always amazes me to watch an athlete transform from struggling-to-get-by to an athlete who rises up out of the ashes and realizes the power of their own thoughts. It's about making the decision to give 100 percent, diving into the process, and having some faith that it will work. Sometimes, a player has to resist and fall into a pit before they "get it," but once they see the light, they can't unsee it. And it doesn't work just on the individual level; the power of positive energy can turn a rag-tag baseball team to successful competitors. The moment you recognize the power you have over your thoughts, over your body, and over the way you play, nothing can stop your forward movement and success.

The moment you recognize the power you have over your thoughts, over your body, and over the way you play, nothing can stop your forward movement and success.

Say YES to Positive Energy

One of my favorite football players is Taysom Hill, who plays for the New Orleans Saints. Hill is one of the most exciting players to watch in the NFL. Sure, his physical abilities are awesome, but witnessing the positive energy he brings to the game and his team is incredible. You can tell he enjoys his job and loves playing the game. No matter what happens, he's always smiling. Even when he's tackled hard by a defender who's talking trash in his face, Hill simply smiles at them and jogs back to the huddle with his teammates to take on the next play. Of course his physical skills make him a huge asset, allowing him to play many positions, but the positive energy he brings to the team and the game is irreplaceable, and that's what makes him so fun to watch. It's also the reason fans love him.

Positive energy like the kind Taysom Hill brings to every game is contagious, but so is negativity. We have a choice every day, every moment, to choose which kind of energy we're going to bring to the table. Problems are inevitable, but we have the ultimate power to stay positive and seek solutions. But we also have the choice to let those around us, our circumstances, and our own lackluster performances dictate a negative outlook that doesn't allow us to see solutions. Which choice do you think gives you more power to live the life you desire?

We have a choice every day, every moment, to choose which kind of energy we're going to bring to the table.

Positive energy is like having money in the bank. When you're tired, defeated, or at a loss for answers, you can go to the bank and withdraw some positive energy. This influx of positive energy gives you the stamina to keep going. It gives you a winner's mindset that refuses to accept defeat, and it gives you the time and brain space you need to think of solutions that will help you do better. A reserve of positive energy that you can tap into at any moment can help you transform from an average athlete and person to an elite athlete and person, ready to take on any issue and accomplish whatever you want.

Positive energy is like having money in the bank.

And don't think your attitude doesn't matter just because you have amazing athletic talent. A friend told me once about how her college team voted off their most talented player during their quest to be in the top ten in the nation. This record-breaking athlete lost a full-ride scholarship based solely on her negative attitude and how it was affecting the other players. Things like showing up late for practices, not giving her all during training sessions, and shrugging her shoulders at everyone like she didn't care added up quickly. The rest of the team noticed that her negative attitude and energy were rubbing off on them. They were less excited about their games, weren't pushing forward, and everyone stopped caring.

Again, like positive energy, negative energy is contagious. So, take stock daily of what you're creating and spreading around. Are you excited to show up to practice every day and look toward the next challenge? Or do you find yourself not really caring if you win or lose? Be honest with yourself and think about why you're feeling whatever it is that you typically feel. If negative energy is impacting your life or your sport, it's time to become aware of it and take action. That's why this daily introspection is so valuable. It might seem like a boring exercise, but it always leads to a better attitude, a better sense of self, and ultimately, a better performance.

Gain that ever-important edge by improving what happens in your mind. What if you were a simple thought away from winning? Wouldn't you consider upgrading your thoughts and adjusting your focus? Picture yourself at a critical moment in your sport where you are face-to-face with your competitor and you really don't have anything over him; you've got a 50/50 chance. You've probably been here before, where the game could go either way, and you likely remember the pressure you felt to win. Now, if I came up to you in that moment and told you that your chances of winning against your opponent could be tipped in your favor if you simply said to yourself, *Remember all the positive energy training you've done? Use it now*, would you do it? I'm pretty sure you would! By harnessing and working with positive energy in addition to the other tools I provide in this book, you can gain a significant edge over your competition.

What if you were a simple thought away from winning? Wouldn't you consider upgrading your thoughts and adjusting your focus?

Here are five of the most important elements of cultivating positive energy that I've experienced over the years
that you can implement immediately to up your mental
game and supercharge your performance.

1. **Focus on what you can control.** It doesn't do you
   any good to focus on your numbers or on winning
   the game. You really can't control that stuff as
   much as you would like to. You can, however,
   control how you perform your duties for your role.
   If you're an outfielder, focus on your role and do
   the job as thoroughly as possible. When you're up
   to bat, focus on your effort one pitch at a time,
   controlling your emotions and looking out for your
   own typical pitfalls along the way.

2. **Always be on the lookout for positives. (There
   are plenty to be found if you just look for them.)**
   Count all the good things you encounter during
   your practices and games. Enjoy your teammates'
   good play, the great weather, the bonding and
   sportsmanship you encounter, and reflect on what
   you did well. Anything negative, evaluate it, figure
   out how to improve it, then move on. And
   remember, some negatives can be flipped into
   positives. For example, "errors = learning." We
   never stop learning, and that it is definitely a
   positive.

3. **Be with positive people and be that positive
   person you would like to hang out with.** Two
   negatives don't make a positive. And no one wakes

up hoping that everyone they encounter that day is spewing pessimism. Therefore, commit to keeping a positive attitude and to helping others cultivate a more optimistic mindset. If your teammate makes a mistake, ask them what they plan on doing differently next time. Ask them if you can help. Someone giving you flack for a bad play? Keep your response positive: "Yeah, that was a tough one. I'm really looking forward to making it good next time."

4. **Challenge your negative thoughts before you finish thinking them.** *That was really stu- ...nope, I got this. I'm good.* Don't even let a negative thought enter in your mind. If it does, track it down and kick it out. It does not belong in your space. Commit to doing this for one week.

Don't even let a negative thought enter in your mind. If it does, track it down and kick it out. It does not belong in your space.

5. **Remember your *why* statement and refer to it every day.** Think back to the *why* statement—the reason you play your sport—that you wrote as part of your Chapter 3 work-up. Your *why* statement says it all: You're here because you love it, and that love overrides all the negatives. Anytime you feel discouraged or tempted to sink

into a negative mindset, think of your *why* statement and let it revive and encourage you.

Now it's time to put all this into action by creating a positive energy statement, your go-to statement that you will use to keep your thoughts aligned with your pursuit of success on and off the field.

1. Copy down your *why* statement here. Even if you have it memorized and have been focusing on it each day, writing something down has the added benefit of burning it into your memory. Then, after you have written your *why* statement, pull out the key words.

   Why statement: _____

   _____

   _____

2. Here's a sample *why* statement that I will break down here: "I play baseball because I like being outside, and I love being on a team yet being able to have my space to perform alone. It also connects me with my family, who loves baseball." Key Words: outside, team, me, family, perform

   Key Words: _____

   _____

   _____

3. Now, use the key words you just identified to form positive energy statements. Use these statements when your energy and motivation are low. They're great for getting revved up pre-game. Example: I'm here to perform. I'm here to be part of the team. I'm here to play outside. I'm here to play for myself. I'm here because it connects me to my family.

Now you try one: I'm here to _____

_____

_____

4. Next you will learn and/or create one more phrase based on your personality type that can help you keep the positive energy flowing. Flip back to Chapter 4 to refresh your memory on your personality profile and circle your three types here: Introvert or Extrovert; Stable/Conscientious or Wired/Neurotic; High-Strung, Low-Key, or Tightly Wound.

   a. Introvert (Use this phrase or rewrite your own): I'm ready to go and ready to connect with my teammates!

   b. Extrovert (Use this phrase or rewrite your own): I'm here for me—no one else.

   c. Stable/Conscientious (Use this phrase or rewrite your own): I'm giving everything I've got today!

   d. Wired/Neurotic (Use this phrase or rewrite your own): I'm calm, and I've got this.

  e. High-Strung: Stay focused.
  f. Low-Key: Now is the time! Right now!
  g. Tightly Wound: I control myself. Nothing controls me.

Be sure to underline or highlight the key phrases for yourself along with your positive energy statement. Then copy them down on a blank piece of paper and post them on your wall. Many athletes have associated their statements or themes for themselves with scripture, mentors, other professional athletes, or even family members they memorialize. Be creative. Dig deep and see what matters most to you and how it can inspire you to show up at your practices, workouts, and games with desire and passion for being the very best.

Coach Tip:

Most of what I suggest to the athletes reading this book is also applicable for coaches (and parents too). Show your athletes that you're just as invested in being the best coach as they are in being the best athletes. Create your own positive energy statements and tape them to the back of your clipboard. Practice using them, say them out loud, and let your athletes see you doing it in practice. Let them see how powerful it can be to stay in control of yourself and emanate positive energy that uplifts you and everyone around you.

Create your own positive energy statements and tape them to the back of your clipboard. Practice using them, say them out loud, and let your athletes see you doing it in practice.

Parent Tip:

Parents, you can do this, too. This exercise is invaluable and will translate into your everyday life, like everything else in this book. When your athlete sees that you have taken the time to create your own positive energy statements, have hung them up in your car and next to the bathroom mirror, and have used them to transform your life, they will be inspired and follow along.

Chapter Work-Up:

When you put forth maximum effort, play with a positive attitude, and keep your spirit strong in the face of adversity, it will lead to powerful outcomes. Right now, write down your positive energy statements and post them wherever you can see them daily. Memorize them and put them to use every time you experience any negative thought or feeling. Remember, you're in control of your experience, so make it positive for yourself and others. At this point, you should have your goals, your confidence statement, and now your positive energy statement posted where you can see them throughout the day. Keep them in your locker, on the mirror, on your door as you head out, and in your car.

PERFORMANCE JOURNAL

CHAPTER NINE

Mental & Physical Toughness

"Concentration and mental toughness are the margins of victory."
—**Bill Russell**

Unfortunately, as a scout, I have seen lots of physically talented young athletes who are mentally and physically soft. Over the past several years, I have witnessed many elite youth teams that are extremely talented, yet they lack the kind of toughness they will need in order to excel. This missing component eventually leads to athletes' not being able to grow beyond the performance they achieved in their youth.

These young athletes walk into the park with their fancy uniforms and expensive rolling bags (that most of the time their mom is rolling for them), and they go out and beat teams 20-0 or 19-2. They are talented and impressive, for sure. But during the course of the game, I often see one of them get hit by a soft curveball and fall to the ground screaming and crying. Mom and Dad sometimes run down to the field to check on their player, disrupting the game. Or one of the players slides into home plate and gets a brush burn, and again, rolls around on the ground crying like they have been seriously wounded. Once again their parents rush down to the field to get their kid a Band-Aid or ice.

I am not trying to criticize parents or ruffle any feathers here. I understand that we all love and care for our children, and it's our job to protect them from harm. The point I want to emphasize is that rushing down to soothe a developing athlete for every minor injury does them no favors. In the long run, you're hurting them worse than their small scrape or bruise. The same goes for letting them text or play games on their phones while you haul their bags for them. A child of eight, nine, or ten is old enough to be responsible for keeping up with their equipment. Giving them small yet manageable tasks like these lay the groundwork for self-confidence, a good work ethic, and so many other qualities that will serve them as they grow.

The point I want to emphasize is that rushing down to soothe a developing athlete for every minor injury does them no favors. In the long run, you're hurting them worse than their small scrape or bruise.

Toughness Comes with the Territory

Mentally and physically weak players cannot play sports at an advanced level. Teach your children to be tough by letting them deal with the temporary and minor pains they encounter on the playing field or on the court. Most minor injuries that occur in sports fall into what I call the "30-Second Rule." It hurts for only 30 seconds. Suck it up, rub some dirt on it, and walk it off. If there is a serious injury, let the coach and their staff of professionals take care of it.

Most minor injuries that occur in sports fall into what I call the "30-Second Rule." It hurts for only 30 seconds. Suck it up, rub some dirt on it, and walk it off.

When they were younger, I would always tell my kids if I ever saw them rolling around on the ground and screaming up a storm, I better see bones sticking out of their skin. I know that sounds harsh, but pain tolerance is an excellent example of mental and physical toughness. Screaming and throwing a fit is best ignored in most cases. They'll stop. (But on the chance that a player sustains a more serious injury, rest assured that the coaches and other staff will immediately take action and ensure that your child is safe.)

Older athletes, I'm talking to you now: Just because you're older now doesn't mean you aren't still "throwing fits" or submitting to negative self-talk that pulls you entirely out of a game. Even though at your age you may no longer be crying on the field, you can benefit from working on your mental and physical toughness just the same.

The bottom line: If you want to be an elite athlete, get familiar with these tools that will help you surmount any obstacle. Here they are:

The 4 Cs: Challenge, Commitment, Control, Confidence

Psychologist Peter Clough has extensively studied the subject of mental toughness, which basically means an athlete's ability to bounce back from adversity. In 2002, Clough and his fellow researchers published the world's first official survey to measure mental toughness, the MTQ48. This online, 48-question psychometric survey measures mental toughness across what he calls "the 4 Cs" on an individual or group level. To access it, visit AQR International at https://aqrinternational.co.uk/mtq48-mental-toughness-questionnaire. If you'd like to learn more about the 4 Cs, Clough's book *Developing Mental Toughness*, written in conjunction with Doug Strycharczyk, is a great resource!

Here's a quick overview of what the 4 Cs mean and how they apply to you. Get a highlighter out or a pen so you can refer back to this essential information that can transform you.

Challenge: To what extent you see challenges, change, adversity, and see variety or different options as opportunities. This means: How you react and feel about something that comes up in your life that challenges you, changes your previous plans or way of doing things. People or situations can come unexpectedly into your life and change your path. Do you see these changes as opportunities to push yourself to make something better out of it?

People or situations can come unexpectedly into your life and change your path. Do you see these changes as opportunities to push yourself to make something better out of it?

Commitment: To what extent you will make promises and the extent to which you will keep those promises. When you promise to be somewhere at a certain time, you show up, no excuses. You don't need excuses because you have thought about and planned for delays that could come up, so you leave early—that is honoring a commitment.

Control: To what extent you believe you shape what happens to you and manage your emotions when doing it. Your sense of control over your environment may seem limited. However, you can adapt to the change by creating your plan and adjust your beliefs and feelings to those plans. Alongside this is your control over your emotions, your reactions to external influences that can suddenly change your plans and cause a disruption. You can't control the fact you were injured, but you can manage your reaction to it.

Confidence: To what extent you believe you have the ability to deal with what you will face and the inner strength to stand your ground when needed. This is pretty straightforward: Do you believe you can deal with changes and adversity based on your inner strength that tells you, *I can do this!* No matter what a person or situation throws at you, your goal is to keep your cool and know deep down that you have what it takes to make something great happen.

No matter what a person or situation throws at you, your goal is to keep your cool and know deep down that you have what it takes to make something great happen.

How you deal with challenges, stressors, and pressure is a key factor in how you perform as an athlete. There are two approaches to dealing with pressure, and both deserve your full attention and practice. Now take the 4 Cs and use them to become an elite athlete.

Preparation is the first approach to being mentally and physically tough, and there are many ways to prepare yourself for the inevitable changes and challenges and how you'll react to them. Practice these habits daily:

1. Challenge: Before you jump out of bed in the morning, roll onto your back and look at the ceiling. Say this morning mantra aloud or quietly to yourself: *I am ready for any challenge. I am committed to my work and my team. I am in control of my reactions. I am confident in my abilities.*

Say this morning mantra aloud or quietly to yourself: I am ready for any challenge. I am committed to my work and my team. I am in control of my reactions. I am confident in my abilities.

2. Commitment: When you make a promise or commit to something or someone, stick to it. Take a moment to think about what it will take today to keep that commitment you made. Maybe you need to set your alarm for an earlier wakeup time so you can run that errand for your grandmother. Maybe you need to take that run in the park since you skipped it the day before.

3. Control: Think before you act. Ask yourself if it's worth it at the moment. After you make a mistake and start to beat yourself up, ask yourself if it's worth the negative commentary in your head. That negative loop will be harder to get rid of the longer it keeps playing in your head. Immediately take control and repeat your morning mantra: *I am ready for any challenge. I am committed to my work and my team. I am in control of my reactions. I am confident in my abilities.* Done.

4. Confidence: Even the most confident athlete loses confidence sometimes, especially when they are faced with what seems to be someone or something they cannot control, whether it's an injury or a competitor seemingly better than them. In Chapters 12-14, techniques are shared that serious athletes use to tap into a place within themselves that is unshakable and strong. Confidence is 100 percent mental, and if you're not strong, it can be stripped away within seconds if you don't practice these techniques and keep

them in your toolbox, ready to use when the time comes...and that time is coming.

Live It. Be It.

Acting out what you practice is the second approach to being mentally and physically tough. It can be challenging to shut down anger or pain that has sunk its teeth in and won't let go. But if you've been practicing the 4 Cs, it will be easier to stop all emotions, and even lessen your pain, in an instant.

Note that physical pain and emotions are a viable mode of communication from your brain and body alerting you to something that has changed and needs attention. Information like shooting pain is not to be ignored, but questioned, observed, then dealt with. Likewise, if your first reaction is anger with your team when you lose a game, it is to be questioned, observed, and dealt with. It signals a problem, so ask, *Why am I angry?* The answer is usually that you are blaming others for a bad performance. You don't control others; you control yourself. Stick with the 4 Cs and share this workbook with your teammates.

With physical injuries, we usually have trained staff to help ask the questions and assess the injury. However, it is essential that you ask yourself important questions as well. Stay calm and ask yourself, *How does this really feel? Where is the pain exactly? Can I stand up?* If you can stand, then get up.

Stay calm and ask yourself, How does this really feel? Where is the pain exactly? Can I stand up? *If you can stand, then get up.*

When you have intense emotions, stop, then ask yourself if it matters at the moment or if you can park it and get back to it later. If someone is in your face and challenging you, ask yourself, *Is it worth it to have a knee-jerk reaction and respond in anger? Is it worth the consequences to my team, my coach, and to myself?*

Get Grit

You are not born with mental strength. You develop it. The mind is more important than the body, and the mind controls the body. Mental training is a vital part of how elite athletes prepare for success. They develop grit, and it serves them throughout their career.

You are not born with mental strength. You develop it.

Grit can be developed and strengthened through intentional practices. Grit is putting one foot in front of the other. Grit is holding fast to a goal you love. It's to invest, minute-to-minute and day-to-day, in challenging practice. Martin Luther King, Jr., said, "The ultimate measure of a man is not where he stands in moments of comfort and convenience, but where he stands at times of challenge and controversy." It's true that character is revealed through sport, because sport will always eventually provide the adversity to test us. Who on your team is mentally tough? Do you have the resilience to thrive in a tough, selfish world full of unlimited forms of adversity? Stay mentally focused and tough and make sure to dig into the chapter work-up.

> *Grit is putting one foot in front of the other. Grit is holding fast to a goal you love. It's to invest, minute-to-minute and day-to-day, in challenging practice.*

Coach Tip:

When you have younger players, it's wise to set some ground rules for injuries, mishaps, and frustrations on the field the first day of the season. Send a letter home to the parents about reinforcing mental and physical toughness and how it's helping their athletes grow up and create self-confidence to dust off the frustration and pain and get up and play the next pitch. Keep in mind the individual personalities of your athletes so you're able to respond with the best action and words when the chips are down, and to get the most out of your athletes and help them grow mentally and physically tougher as the season progresses. Be sure to visit their goals with them and add some to their list. For example, one goal you might help them set is to come in first when doing running drills. Or that when they get hurt or frustrated, they take off their cap and dust off their pants and spend some time readjusting their cap while quietly repeating their confidence phrase (the goal being they do this every single time without fail).

Parent Tip:

Reinforce with your athlete that they are in control of their emotions and can push their bodies farther than they presently push themselves, because they can. Step back and let the coach do their job, and allow your athlete to work out their own solutions and live through the tough moments. There is no other way to create self-confidence than by stepping up and solving your problems with your own will and determination. Intervening too often takes away their ability to problem-solve and enjoy their successes. Instead, support them by working on your own mental and physical toughness and walking a similar path that they are walking as they adopt the philosophies in this book. Show them what it looks like to brush off the stuff that knocks us down and get up to accomplish our goals for the day. Remember, push yourself—not your athlete. As they watch you live out the principles of mental and physical toughness, they will be more inclined to do the same on their own.

There is no other way to create self-confidence than by stepping up and solving your problems with your own will and determination.

Chapter Work-Up:

1. Copy down the morning mantra you learned earlier in this chapter below, and while doing so, feel what it's like to make good on promises and follow through. Feel what it's like to be confident in your abilities. _____

   _____

   _____

2. Create your own mantra to repeat when you face a challenge. Make it short, make it memorable, and most importantly, create one that you can feel energize you on the inside. And remember, fake it until you make it. You will make it happen; just keep at it daily. _____

   _____

   _____

3. Write down a time when you injured yourself to the point where you were unsure if you could play again. Do you feel like you have a good gauge

of pain? Can you control your pain and discomfort? Write down your thoughts here, and your plan for the next time you are challenged and what you will do to overcome it. _____

_____

_____

This takes you directly into the next chapter on resilience and adversity, where you're going to work on being able to overcome any obstacle that's thrown at you. You're going to learn how to make chicken salad out of what can seem like chicken poop.

PERFORMANCE JOURNAL

CHAPTER TEN

Resilience & Overcoming Adversity

"Obstacles don't have to stop you. If you run into a wall, don't turn around and give up. Figure out how to climb it, go through it, or work around it."

—Michael Jordan

There are so many great athletes who get robbed of using their abilities when game-time adversities overtake them. They end up just keeping up with the game, not competing. Upset that they aren't the superstar they wanted to be, they end up in slumps after losing out to distractions either in their head or coming from the crowd. Powerful, elite athletes are effective because they bring their positive and resilient mindsets to the game. They are able to do so because they have worked on it just as much as they work out in the gym. They focus on their goals, desire, work ethic, and their *why* and bring these aspects of themselves to the field every time.

Why are these things so important? Because sports and the games we play are filled with unpredictable momentum changes. Momentum can swing from one team to the other or one player to another in a split second—it's out of your control. Bad things are going to happen in sports. You will drop the ball and make a bad play. Despite that, the goal is to control what you can—your reaction. Adversity is inevitable. It's how you handle the adversity that determines champions and mentally tough athletes. Injuries are also common in sports. Being able to bounce back both physically and mentally from injury is determined by resilience, or the athlete's "bouncebackability."

Adversity is inevitable. It's how you handle the adversity that determines champions and mentally tough athletes.

Resilience is defined as your capability to deal with stress and adversity. Adversity is a difficulty you are faced with. How do you deal with difficult situations you've found yourself in?

You twist your ankle in a game. After taking a deep breath and giving yourself several calm seconds to analyze your body without submitting to emotions, you realize that you are not badly hurt, and that you are able to walk it off and focus entirely on the next play. That's resilience. That's overcoming adversity. That's bouncebackability.

There are many techniques to becoming resilient and overcoming adversity, and (no surprise here) each of these are directly linked to your thoughts or mindset. And that entails readjusting your goals, surrounding yourself with good people, using visualization to prepare for adversity, and practicing self-regulation, where you take what you learned about mental toughness in the last chapter and implement it.

There are many techniques to becoming resilient and overcoming adversity, and (no surprise here) each of these are directly linked to your thoughts or mindset.

Remember that grit, perseverance, and resilience are developed, created, made, and strengthened through intentional daily practice. If you are doing your exercises daily, when you do hit a major setback, you'll be ready to tackle it head-on. You won't be wasting time on doubt or worry. You will experience only a steadfast and intense desire to move past the obstacle and become a better athlete once you tackle it.

Using Self-Regulation to Overcome Adversity and Build Resilience

Self-regulation is the core of sport psychology. Self-regulation is the ability to control your thoughts, emotions, and motivations. Take into account what you can control and what you can't. You can't help if you pulled your tendon, even if it could have been avoided. It's done. It's time to move on. The key to mastering self-regulation lies in focusing entirely on the moment you're in now, and in finding solutions and implementing them immediately, and daily. Your pulled tendon will be the reason you become an elite athlete. Why? Because your mind leads your body, not the other way around.

The key to mastering self-regulation lies in focusing entirely on the moment you're in now, and in finding solutions and implementing them immediately, and daily.

Picture this: You're on the field, and a questionable call from the ump ends your chance at bat. You had it in your heart and mind that you were going to knock one out of the park that day, and the ump took that dream away from you. The next decision you make reflects your ability to self-regulate and overcome adversity. Notice I used the word "decision." You have a choice. A choice in how you react to adversity and things not going your way. You have a decision every time to act negatively or positively. This is all part of mental toughness, and you are starting to build that muscle right now as you dedicate yourself to reading this book, doing the activities, and making them a daily routine.

You have a choice. A choice in how you react to adversity and things not going your way. You have a decision every time to act negatively or positively.

Prepare yourself now for adversity (because, as we've established, it is a certainty in sports and in life). We go over this in more detail in Chapter 13. The best way to prepare yourself for issues that will inevitably pop up is to visualize how you'll react in those moments. How do you want to handle the bad call, the annoying guy in the stands, the teammate who's having a bad game, or even a possible injury?

Visualize yourself on the ground after a collision with a teammate. Not only are you in pain, but you can't stop the wetness in your eyes, and that has you even more anxious than any injury. Visualize yourself solving the problem calmly: You pull your cap down over your eyes and hold your hand up to anyone coming to help. Repeat what you're saying to yourself in your head to overcome the emotions you know aren't helpful: *I'm all good. I'm strong. I've got this.*

Repeat what you're saying to yourself in your head to overcome the emotions you know aren't helpful: I'm all good. I'm strong. I've got this.

Visualization like this can help prepare you for adversity and take the stress out of the situation, so when something similar unfolds in real life, you can rally more quickly and do so in the most positive way for you and your teammates. You'll notice that even if you practice for an incident that never happens, it helps you prepare for other incidents because you've already started the positive recovery process.

To continue overcoming more long-term adversity, like an injury or being placed on a team you don't want to be on, you must readjust your goals and surround yourself with good, positive people who can help you. In the case of being injured, you might find yourself needing to vent and so you spew out a bunch of negativity to someone. Make sure that someone can sit and listen quietly, and empathize with you but will not help you dig a deeper hole of negativity. Choose someone who is strong and mature enough to tell you when it's time to turn those feelings into something more positive.

Let's look at the second example: You got placed on a team you think is beneath your talent. One friend loves commiserating with you, and soon they have got you so worked up that you're ready to quit the team. While it's fine to remain friends with this person, they are not the best person to turn to right now. But a different, older friend comes to mind—one who is right about things so often that it can be annoying. The thing is, you know this friend won't let you get emotional and dig a hole so deep you can't get out of it. Be sure to surround yourself with people like this, those who can offer solutions or at least keep you positive so you can create your own solutions.

Above all, remember that you have a choice when you're facing serious adversity. Your choices are (1) to dig your hole and let it drag you down for months or (2) to get a mindset of strength and positivity and get the issue solved immediately so you can enjoy success for the next several months instead. These solutions will help.

As I mentioned in Chapter 5, the goals you created are a living thing and they need to be revisited several times a year. Whenever changes brought on by adversity or other circumstances enter your life, check back in with your goals and determine whether they need adjustment. If you come away with a pulled tendon, it's time to add goals for your recovery, short- and long-term. If you lose your playing position and need to earn it back, reset your goals to match your plan and build the desire to compete for your position.

Whenever changes brought on by adversity or other circumstances enter your life, check back in with your goals and determine whether they need adjustment.

If you learned in Chapter 4 that you are wired, high-strung, or tightly wound, you might lean toward perfectionism. You may not keep your room clean all the time, but perfectionism can come out screaming in sports. Do you take mistakes too seriously and beat yourself up a lot for making them? Does it irritate you when things aren't done exactly as you think they should be? Do you get upset easily with teammates who don't do their part? You might be a perfectionist. You need to take the bathtub test.

Put two inches of water in your bathtub and step into it with both feet. If you can stand on top of the water, it's okay to demand perfection of yourself. If your feet come to rest on the bottom of the tub, however, what you've always known is obvious...you are not perfect.

Yeah, that was kind of a trick, but you get my point. When you revisit your goals, make sure to adjust them so they can be reached; this will allow you to feel some success. Also, give extra attention and practice to the techniques that will be taught in Chapter 14 and those that were taught in Chapter 8. Learn how to relax before games, so you're not so tightly wound and anxious that you can't even perform. Then use the creation of positive energy to win over every perceived loss.

Learn how to relax before games, so you're not so tightly wound and anxious that you can't even perform. Then use the creation of positive energy to win over every perceived loss.

Striving for perfection is admirable, and I encourage you to utilize the focus and desire needed to improve, but perfection itself is not a healthy measure of success for anyone. Players who must have perfection at all costs will tie themselves into knots if they don't get a hit every time, or if they fail to hit their target with each pitch. Be sure to give yourself permission to not be perfect and welcome the mistakes. Remember, mistakes are information that you can learn from. We need information if we're going to grow and be better. So let them come, and you'll overcome them. The freer you feel when you're competing, the more likely you are to play your best.

Be sure to give yourself permission to not be perfect and welcome the mistakes. Remember, mistakes are information that you can learn from.

When you do make a mistake, take a step back from your mistake and examine it as someone else might see it. Go ahead and imagine that whatever real or perceived failure happened not to you, but to your best friend on the team. What would you say to him? Distancing yourself from the emotions of failing makes it easier to learn the lesson it's teaching you. Ask yourself, *How can this experience help me become a better player?*

Distancing yourself from the emotions of failing makes it easier to learn the lesson it's teaching you. Ask yourself, How can this experience help me become a better player?

For those who trend toward introversion or scored low-key or low-ambition earlier in the book, it's important to connect with how it would feel to stand on water. It's the feeling you get when you're water skiing, snow skiing, or doing a flip on a trampoline. It's that freeing feeling that makes your scalp tingle, that feeling of letting go and enjoying what it feels like to play the game for fun. This is exactly what you need to tap into to drive up your ambition, amp up your positive energy, and connect with your team.

When you do have one of these uplifting, "heck, yeah!" moments, stop for a minute and lock it into your memory. Take a moment to go through exactly how it feels. Later on that night, after this great experience, recall it as you fall asleep and bring forth those feelings once again. Do you remember the smells around you? What your surroundings looked like? How it felt? Even how it tasted? Cultivate cues you can bring back, like landmarks, to show you the way back to that positive experience. Bring the experience back whenever you want or need to bring energy and positivity back into your life. This recall is great for pregame time and will make even more sense in Chapter 13.

Following is a system I use with athletes to help them benefit from moments of failure and make them even better athletes than had they not dropped the ball. Failure is feedback. Nothing more.

"There is too much at stake to spend time being upset. You must develop the ability to learn from what just happened, then forgive yourself for doing it and forget that it happened. Learn, forgive, and forget: Once you have done this, you have done all you can do."
—Dr. Curt Tribble, Heart Surgeon

When you lift weights, you build muscle to hit the ball farther. When you work on developing resilience, you can overcome the anxiety of batting against an outstanding pitcher. Like building up the biceps in your arm, you build your mental muscle to overcome anxiety. That means you *need* adversity in order to practice dealing with it as effectively as possible. Even though it is daunting, you *want* that bigger-than-life pitcher throwing, because deep down you want to know what it's like to hit against the best. So, when you see adversity headed your way, tell adversity to bring it—you're ready to build your mental muscles.

When you see adversity headed your way, tell adversity to bring it—you're ready to build your mental muscles.

Here is a system I share with players on how to get past failure and adversity. It can be adapted to any sport.

1. Take a breath. Take a couple of deep breaths and make sure your muscles relax.

2. Use your focal point. Go back to trusting yourself on the next pitch. Restart.

3. Take off your glove or hat. When the glove or cap is off, you can be disgusted.

4. When the glove or cap goes back on, however, it means you are ready to focus on the next pitch. Stop trying to control anything outside of yourself. You can't control what happens around you, but you can control how you choose to respond. You can't control the ump, your teammates or your coach, or even the crowd.

5. Take back control of yourself. You must be in control of yourself before you can control your performance. You can control your attitude, effort, thoughts, and emotions. When you consistently control your thoughts and reactions, you'll begin to feel powerful, and it will catch on to the point that you'll glide right past temporary setbacks. You'll make your own luck, mastering your nerves and making your next play a show of excellence.

When you develop the ability to control yourself in the heat of battle, you are fully in control of yourself, and this mastery that allows you to make good decisions and tap into your best mechanics will help you become an elite athlete.

Coach Tip:

Your job is to develop both the physical and mental ability of your athletes. To teach your athletes resilience in the face of adversity, you need to first create the environment. That means you need to be resilient, have grit, stay late, and push yourself hard. This shows your athletes that you're invested, too. Create an environment that promotes mental toughness and teaches athletes to pull themselves up after falling down. Teach your athletes that momentary failures are gifts. We learn from them, recover from them physically and mentally, and then we have the knowledge to do better next time. Share stories of when you've failed and then rallied. Be honest about moments when you made an error. Tell your athletes what you learned and how you will do better next time.

Teach your athletes that momentary failures are gifts. We learn from them, recover from them physically and mentally, and then we have the knowledge to do better next time.

Additionally, create safe environments in which your athletes can fail, get up, and own the ability to overcome adversity and perform even better. This is the best way to let an athlete own their self-confidence. There's nothing worse than praising a naturally talented athlete and allowing them to rest on their talents. Soon, those talents will be underutilized, and other athletes with a greater work ethic and greater resilience will surpass them. But be sure not to do the opposite either, pushing talented players to the brink of breakdown and making them carry the burden of the entire team. There is a happy medium; be sure to find it.

Parent Tip:

Your job is to create an environment that allows your young athlete to fall, allows them to calmly review the situation, and allows them to create solutions while you encourage them with questions, active listening, and patience. Encourage them to review their goals, adjust them, and continue dedicating themselves daily to fulfill them. But be sure to do this without breathing down their neck. One way to be helpful without becoming a nag is to have them put reminders on their digital calendars for such things as reviewing goals, signing up for training sessions, and so forth. That way their phone is the nag, not you.

Lastly, remember that no matter how quiet or how little your child talks to you, they will inevitably show you their true mood. They'll be laughing with their friends one minute, but as soon as they're inside the house, they're brooding. That's because they feel safe to feel their true feelings out loud at home. Let them feel those feelings. Let them struggle with an obstacle, and let them know you're there for support. Create a safe environment for them to struggle and fail, providing them with the tools taught here in this book to create their own solutions so they can own their success. There's nothing better for naturally creating self-confidence in any human being.

Chapter Work-Up:

Think of a past bad experience. Don't overthink it. Write down the first one that pops into your head. Now, come up with three reasons that this bad experience was actually good for you. It can be tough at first, especially if the experience was your grandmother going to the hospital with a health issue. Keep working at seeing the good. Maybe the experience helped your grandmother see it was time to take better care of herself, or that she realized she can start eating healthier and live longer. Or perhaps the experience helped you notice how you now feel more connected to her and dedicated to keeping her healthy. That's a good thing, and she'll feel that care and connection more than before.

Go ahead and practice this skill whenever any adversity or "bad" things happen. Remember that these "bad" situations are good, because they provide you the opportunity to practice your mental toughness. Even when you are unable to figure out how it can be turned into something good, you have empowered yourself. Situations and other people don't rule over you. You control your reactions and how you see situations and the people in them. Have faith that whatever seems bad can be good—that it is good and that despite the fact that you can't see it yet, your patience will pay off with the answers you need to make your situation better.

This is how you cope with adversity. And there's nothing more important for pregame preparation than to deal with adversity. I could probably write an entire book about this often-overlooked component of pregame mental preparation. With experience, athletes learn how to cope with any adversity—with situations that could cause them to lose focus, confidence, or composure.

If you haven't yet experienced many adverse situations, you'll have to anticipate the challenges that might affect your mindset and develop strategies to cope with each. Your goal is to be prepared mentally for anything that may happen in competition, like an injury or dropping the ball, and to be able to cope effectively.

The most important way of dealing with adversity is by playing in the now, the present moment where the ball starts moving slower. In the now, you can see what you need to do next with more clarity and confidence, and you feel calm, yet ready to strike. In the next chapter, you'll learn what it takes to play the next pitch like a champion.

PERFORMANCE JOURNAL

CHAPTER ELEVEN

Competing in the NOW

"The team that is the most focused and executes the best is the team that wins. That's usually the team that can handle the pressure of the situation."
—Michael Strahan

"Winners live in the present tense. People who come up short are consumed with the future or past. I want to be living in the now."
—Alex Rodriguez

Imagine you're in the middle of a league game. Can you visualize what it's like to be in that very moment when the ball is thrown and to track its movement exactly?

Nothing else matters—no past failure, no future what-ifs, just the ball coming, and you knowing exactly what to do.

In order for you to be able to focus on the physical aspects of the game like this, it is necessary to live in the present. It's difficult to play your best if you're upset about the ump's last call against you, hecklers in the crowd, or if you're worried about your next play and whether you can even pull it off.

Competing in the now is a skill that is useful both on the field and off the field. It helps anyone improve their mental awareness and their ability to focus on the play at hand. When we allow doubt to creep into our minds, usually it's because we are thinking about something in the past or a future worry. This takes away from your being able to perform at your best, so the goal is getting your mind in the present moment, where everything slows down a little, and you're in control.

> *Competing in the now is a skill that is useful both on the field and off the field. It helps anyone improve their mental awareness and their ability to focus on the play at hand.*

Take, for example, a running back who fumbles the ball and the opposing team runs it back for an easy touchdown. The RB is devastated and replays the scene over and over again in his mind. *How could I have done that? I should have done this. I could have done that.* Then he starts worrying about future consequences. *What if we lose the game because of me? If we lose by a touchdown, it will be my fault. If we lose, it means I let the whole team down.*

This common type of thinking only magnifies the negative thoughts and feelings and creates immense pressure on you. It usually leads to more errors. As Alex Rodriguez pointed out in the above quote, winners live in the present tense. Their minds are entirely on the ball, not in the stands with the crowd or trying to figure out how to win.

Luckily, living in the present is a skill that can be practiced anywhere and anytime. At any moment, you can start to feel stress, pressure, or any other sort of negative emotion. There are four very specific and useful tips you can use when you notice something dragging you into the past or the future. Whether you're at practice and about to strike out, or are worrying about failing a previous exam just before you take a new one, these techniques can bring you into the present moment so you can experience peak performance.

Take a Deep Breath

Take a moment right now and take a deep breath—a down-to-your-belly kind of a deep breath that forces you to breathe out in a rush. Push air down into your lungs until they can't take anymore, then let it out. If it helps, you can close your eyes. Go ahead and practice this now.

Use Your Senses to Tune into the Present Moment

Next, allow yourself to utilize your five senses to bring you back into the moment at hand. The present moment is where your power lies. Instead of thinking about past mistakes or future consequences, focus on how you're going to overcome whatever obstacle you're facing. If at any moment you start to feel stress, pressure, or any other sort of negative emotion, pause and take a deep breath. Instead of thinking about what mistakes brought you to the present moment, or what the consequences of the future might be, focus on how you're going to overcome whatever obstacle you're facing.

The present moment is where your power lies. Instead of thinking about past mistakes or future consequences, focus on how you're going to overcome whatever obstacle you're facing.

During your next competition, feel the vibration of the water as your competitors swim in the lanes next to you. Hear the roar of the crowd as you step up to the free-throw line. See the dimples on the golf ball sitting on the tee. Feel the seams of the baseball as you wind up for your next pitch. Taste the sweat and blood as you step into the ring for the tenth round. Smell the fresh-cut grass on the gridiron. Allowing your mind to *experience* all the sensations of performing in a sport will help keep you grounded in the present. While this exercise can be practiced anywhere, anytime, it's best to try to implement this during your practices and competition. Live in the present, and the results will ensue.

Allowing your mind to experience *all the sensations of performing in a sport will help keep you grounded in the present.*

Listen to Your Self-Talk

It's also important to check-in with your self-talk. If you've never stopped for a moment to notice that voice in your head, here's your chance. If you have, let's do an experiment and see what your self-talk is up to right now. You need to know, and it helps with how you'll move forward.

Sit in a quiet place and set a timer for five minutes. Close your eyes and picture a blank piece of paper. At first, your thoughts will be all over the place. When your mind wanders, remind yourself to see the blank piece of paper once again, pulling yourself back over and over again if necessary.

When time is up, reflect on the experience. Were your thoughts negative or positive? Were you calm and happy about this experiment, or were you annoyed? Did you make it through the entire five minutes? Now that you've listened to your inner voice, you should be able to determine if that voice was positive (patient, enjoying the process) or negative (impatiently waiting for it to be over or annoyed and ready to move forward).

For those who were annoyed or impatient, this is very normal and means you are ready to practice self-talk techniques that are taught more in-depth in Chapter 12. Stay motivated and practice as often as you can, telling yourself what you want to be thinking, what you'd like to be focused on, and working to keep it positive.

Stay motivated and practice as often as you can, telling yourself what you want to be thinking, what you'd like to be focused on, and working to keep it positive.

Those who enjoyed the five-minute exercise are ready to incorporate new levels of discipline by leveling-up to self-talk that leads to purposeful imagery. Make sure your motivation levels stay high by always keeping your goals at the forefront of your thoughts.

What's so amazing about self-talk and mastering these techniques is that you can completely control your emotions and your reactions to anything that happens around you. It's an incredibly powerful technique that will give you an edge in competition. The ability to yank yourself out of a slump by merely pulling your thoughts back to the present moment is what makes the difference between average or good athletes and elite athletes. Do you want to be the player who flies off the handle at a bad call or the player who stays calm and knows they are more than one call, showing up the next moment to win the game?

Do you want to be the player who flies off the handle at a bad call or the player who stays calm and knows they are more than one call, showing up the next moment to win the game?

Fake It 'Til You Make It

Finally, this leads us to "act out what you know is best." This is akin to "fake it until you make it." To begin acting out what you want to feel and experience for yourself, you must start by bringing yourself to the present moment. Tell yourself that you "got this" and snap back into the here-and-now. Hustle to your next spot like you're a champion. Hold your head up, shoulders back, and give a nod to the coach that your head is still in the game. And don't worry—it all gets easier with time and practice.

To master these fundamental skills, continually practice these techniques and tailor-fit them for your personality and lifestyle. Practice the breathing, the senses, the self-talk, and act how you know is best several times a day. Do it until it becomes an automatic response to anything that wants to pull you into "what if I" or "that was" mode. This will enable you to be in control of yourself all of the time. That's the mind and behavior of an elite athlete.

Practice the breathing, the senses, the self-talk, and act how you know is best several times a day. Do it until it becomes an automatic response to anything that wants to pull you into "what if I" or "that was" mode.

The skill of competing in the present is not something that happens overnight. It takes years of mental training and learning how to truly embrace failure in order to master competing in the now. Having a "reset word" that you keep in your head can help reset your mind to focus on the next play or the next pitch. Breathing techniques and visualization are also helpful ways to reset your mind to focus on the present.

Raising My Own Mentally Tough Athlete

I have worked with thousands of athletes on both the mental and physical aspects of sports, but none more often than my own children. Mentally tough athletes or performers are a treat to watch as they compete. And watching my oldest son, Drake, grow and learn year after year about how to compete in the moment has truly been impressive.

As soon as Drake was old enough to hold a ball and bat, I began teaching him the importance of embracing failure. The first quote I shared with him and told him to remember was a quote from Barry Bonds: "You will never enjoy success until you can learn to forget your failures." I think Drake was about six years old when I first told him that quote. He's now a 21-year-old college athlete, and he still has that same quote listed on his social media profiles.

As soon as Drake was old enough to hold a ball and bat, I began teaching him the importance of embracing failure. The first quote I shared with him and told him to remember was a quote from Barry Bonds: "You will never enjoy success until you can learn to forget your failures."

When Drake was young, I helped him decide on a reset word and a physical focal point to help him reset his mind anytime he was distracted with negativity or stress. His focal point was the foul pole on a baseball field, and the reset word he chose was "beastmode," which is (a) the action of stepping up and destroying the competition, and (b) a superhuman state of mind in which animal instinct takes over the mind and body. Every athlete can come up with their unique reset word and their own focal point depending on what sport they play.

The first time I realized Drake understood the concept of competing in the now and embracing failure was when he was nine years old. It was the first time he stepped on the mound in a kid-pitch game. He did okay for the first three innings, but in the next inning, he hit two batters in a row. The first pitch hit a player in the back, and the second one hit a player in the head.

When I went out to talk to him, I figured he would be shaken up. I asked him if he was tired and if he needed to come out. He looked up at me and said, "No, sir, I know what I'm doing wrong. I am about to strike this son-of-a-b!&@# out."

At that moment, I felt conflicted. Part of me knew I needed to fuss at him and correct him for using that type of language at such a young age. But the other part of me wanted to pat him on the butt and say, "Heck, yeah, that's what I'm talking about, son." Drake did strike out the next two batters and got out of the inning. We did have a conversation about his language after the game, but my point is that he didn't stress about hitting the batters. He shook it off and simply competed with the next pitch, and he was successful.

There were many times throughout his young career that Drake struggled mentally or failed during high-pressure situations and got down on himself. He wouldn't be human if he didn't. But the mental training he has consistently practiced in life and sport has helped his playing career.

While competing during his junior year of high school in the state championship tournament, I again witnessed Drake's mental training working to give him an edge. His team was facing a rival team with a good left-handed pitcher who had recently committed to a Division I college. Hitting in the 2-hole of the batting order, Drake's first two at-bats were a weak ground ball and a strikeout. During his third AB, they intentionally walked the leadoff hitter to get to Drake with two outs and runners on first and second base. Again, Drake hit a weak fly ball into left field to strand the runners.

So, going into the bottom of the last inning, with the game tied 0-0 with two outs, and the winning run standing on second base, Drake came up to the plate for the fourth time in the game. As he walked up to the plate, I remember sitting in the stands with a nervous feeling in my stomach and asking myself, *Is he going to be worried about his last three plate appearances? Is the cheering crowd going to put too much pressure on him?*

As he walked up to the plate, I remember sitting in the stands with a nervous feeling in my stomach and asking myself, Is he going to be worried about his last three plate appearances? Is the cheering crowd going to put too much pressure on him?

The other pitcher was still dominating, hitting his spots and painting the corners. The first pitch came, and Drake took it for a strike on the outside corner. That's when I noticed it. Drake wasn't fazed at all by the crowd or thinking about his last at-bats. He stepped out of the box and stared down at the foul pole. He readjusted his batting gloves (another way of mentally resetting for the next pitch), and he looked down at the tape on his wrist, where the word "beast-mode" was written.

That's when I noticed it. Drake wasn't fazed at all by the crowd or thinking about his last at-bats.

At that moment, the nervous feeling in my stomach disappeared. I knew that Drake's chances of coming through in this clutch situation had just improved exponentially. It was all thanks to his mental training and his dedication to practicing it all those years. He had that look of pure determination on his face as he stepped back into the box. On the next pitch, he laced a line drive into left field as the runner on second base raced around third and slid safe into home with a walk-off 1-0 victory and the 2016 state championship.

The win was great, and it felt amazing, but what was most important was Drake's ability to step away from the crowd. The real prize was the way he let go of the past plays and the talented pitcher on the mound, so he could take a stand in the box with laser focus on that ball and make chicken salad from what could have been a helping of chicken poop.

The real prize was the way he let go of the past plays and the talented pitcher on the mound, so he could take a stand in the box with laser focus on that ball and make chicken salad from what could have been a helping of chicken poop.

When you're face-to-face with your adversity—when you are about to make the decision to cave into the deflating moment of missing a ball—it helps to dig deep and remember your *why*. Repeat the reason you're there, then feel that reason rise in you, straightening your back, pulling your shoulders up, and bringing that feeling of purpose into your chest. This will cut out the distracting noise of errors and negative self-talk and place you back into the moment. Be so clear on why you are there playing that adversity will step aside and let you through. Your *why* is the foundation of the game, so let it prop you back up to take the next pitch.

Be so clear on why you are there playing that adversity will step aside and let you through. Your why is the foundation of the game, so let it prop you back up to take the next pitch.

Coach Tip:

Players must know their job. Any sign that they aren't clear on their role means you need to coach them on it again. Also, make sure you're aware of their best learning style, so you know they will understand every aspect of their job and what it looks like to do it well. They need to be alert and be aware always. This allows them to shut down the doubting voice in their head and get back into the moment.

Work with each of your players to create their "reset word" and to select a physical object they can fix their eye on and remind them the only thing they have control over is that very moment. Whatever ignites that laser focus back on the game for the athlete is important. Train them to use it during practices, as well as games. Additionally, create your reset word and object. Share with your players how you use these techniques and what they can do for them. Remember, all of these techniques need to be practiced day-in and day-out to be effective.

> *Work with each of your players to create their "reset word" and to select a physical object they can fix their eye on and remind them the only thing they have control over is that very moment.*

Parent Tip:

It's best that you practice dropping into the NOW and the other exercises in this book along with your athlete. It creates buy-in from them and reinforces how valuable these techniques are to use in everyday life. These sport psychology techniques are indeed beneficial for everyone, for every circumstance life gives you. By participating in these skill sets daily, you will notice how your life improves along with your athlete's life. When you are both practicing, you will connect better and be able to share your thoughts and successes. Ultimately, it motivates your athlete to participate and engage daily, which in turn helps them to be the best athlete and person they can be.

Chapter Work-Up:

Living and playing in the present is a skill that can be practiced anytime and anywhere. The moment you feel stress or pressure, take a deep breath, check-in with your five senses, and master your self-talk. Practice these techniques; don't just read about them. They will be less effective in your next game if you haven't already been using them at practice or during your daily activities. Most importantly, carry your *why* with you everywhere. Remember what playing felt like way back in Little League or t-ball? Reclaim that feeling in your heart and mind, because that's what the game is about. Remembering how fun it was to learn how to play your sport is one way to get your motivation and energy rolling. There's more to come in the next chapter on shutting the door on negative self-talk and learning to replace it with more effective positive self-talk.

It's time to begin creating your in-game routines. Watch your favorite players closely and see if you can pick up some of their physical routines that may include adjusting their cap just-so, or tapping their bat three times before every pitch. Maybe they tug on their glove where something personal and inspiring is written.

When you're at practice, use something that fits well with who you are, something that can be quickly done, something that's not distracting for others to see, and something that makes you comfortable. Write down some ideas on the clipboard page at the end of this chapter. List some of your current in-game routines and consider whether you need to change your current ones to signify the changes you're making to become a mental master. Be sure to incorporate your confidence statement into your routines to keep your mind and body connected while you do them.

PERFORMANCE JOURNAL

CHAPTER TWELVE

Motivation & Positive Self-Talk

"The difference between the impossible and the possible lies in a man's determination."
—Tommy Lasorda

Why are you reading this book right now? Take a second and answer that question. Why *are* you reading this book right now?

As an athlete, motivation is your reason. It's why you're here reading this right now, why you show up to practice, and why you play the sports you choose. What's your reason for playing sports? Why do you practice your sports? In answering these questions, you'll be able to identify your motivations and then get to the root of your motivation so you can tap into it every day, whether you're at work, in school, or on the field.

Positive self-talk is the key that unlocks motivation. Though it sounds simple enough, positive self-talk is a skill that must be practiced daily—before the morning push-ups, during the push-ups, on and off the field, and before your eyes close for the night. It is more than forcing good thoughts into your head. It's living them.

> *Positive self-talk is the key that unlocks motivation.*

Exploring Intrinsic and Extrinsic Motivation

Let's take a look at your motivation first. Then we can work on kicking your thoughts into gear so you can utilize your motivation. There are two types of motivation: intrinsic and extrinsic. Intrinsic motivation is natural and originates from within. Extrinsic motivation operates from the outside and is not natural to the person. You need both types, and you can use both.

> *Intrinsic motivation is natural and originates from within. Extrinsic motivation operates from the outside and is not natural to the person.*

Have you ever been caught up in the rush of being in the crowd at a concert? How about being in the frenzy of celebrating a win with your team? It is a huge rush, and it motivates us to get up the next day and practice so we can win the next game and feel that positive rush again. That's extrinsic motivation, and it's a great way to work toward goals.

Have you ever visited another city or been out in nature and were curious to find out what you could see if you climbed that rock or wall? We've all been there; curious, and feeling motivated to see the fireworks or see how far we could go. That's intrinsic motivation. It's something we feel inside that gets us to make a move and try something out. We're curious by nature, even competitive by nature, and this is what causes us to build and create new things every day.

Tapping into both of these types of motivations is extremely important if you want to be an elite athlete. When you're coming back from being sick, or when you just lost a game, and have zero motivation to attend practice, this is when you employ both intrinsic and extrinsic motivation techniques to get back out there again. Here are some ideas to practice for yourself.

Tapping into both of these types of motivations is extremely important if you want to be an elite athlete.

Take your list of goals and add an activity to it that's outside of your sport. Maybe you want to take your mountain bike out and hit a new trail you heard about. How about the new rock climbing gym in town you were thinking might be kind of fun? Have you been curious about a topic you want to learn more about, like what causes tornadoes? Write down several of these activities and find room for them on your calendar. Make them happen. You'll notice that in crossing these goals off your list, you're building intrinsic motivation. Satisfy your curiosity and boost your motivation every chance you get!

Next, you want to tap into extrinsic motivation. You might do this by starting a new warm-up routine with your teammates. Create a new mix of music and play it at the beginning of practice.

Snuffing Out the Negative and Replacing It with Positive Self-Talk

To increase motivation and make sure it's there when you need it, practice positive self-talk. What do you say to yourself after you do something wrong while you're playing? It's probably not very gentle or kind. You might be surprised to know that every single person has similar negative thoughts to yours. We all think things like, *That was stupid.* Or, *Why did I do that again?*

> *You might be surprised to know that every single person has similar negative thoughts to yours. We all think things like,* That was stupid. *Or,* Why did I do that again?

These types of thoughts are so automatic, so intrinsic, that it takes a concerted effort and diligent and consistent practice to snuff them out. And even then, years later, they still pop up on occasion. But the good news is, with a little effort and regular practice, your thoughts will quickly revert back to more positive and productive thinking. Here's what you can do:

The first step in rehabilitating your thoughts is recognition. You can't fix what you don't notice, so next time you have a bout of adversity, notice the thoughts that naturally come to mind. If you're having a hard time catching them, sit down and write them out. State the problem you're having and capture what you think about it on paper. Your true thoughts will eventually leak out into what you write. When you get better at automatically recognizing your thoughts, you'll be able to take the next step.

The second step is kicking out the negative thought. I often tell my players to refuse it at the door, like you would a knocking enemy who wants to come in and trash your house. Your mind is your house, and you need to guard it. Say no to the negative thought; tell it to go away.

Your mind is your house, and you need to guard it. Say no to the negative thought; tell it to go away.

The third step is replacing the negative thought with a positive, more encouraging and confidence-enhancing thought. Tell yourself, *I've got this, and I can get it right this time. I will do it, and I will do it now.*

If you're in a particularly tough situation and your mind is a tornado of negativity tossing around every bad move you've ever made, employ the techniques in Chapters 8 and 11. Then replace all that garbage with the tools you have right now, like breathing deeply and calming down. Use this very moment to gain your control back and start feeding yourself positive thoughts that will get you back in the game. *I can do this. I am doing this because I'm an exceptional athlete.*

Use this very moment to gain your control back and start feeding yourself positive thoughts that will get you back in the game.

Is it hard to believe what you're trying to feed yourself? Sometimes, when you feel lower than usual, trying to tell yourself, *I'm a great player* seems laughable and it won't work in the moment. Do it anyway and keep at it. It's like lightly twisting your ankle. It seems to hurt bad, but if you keep walking and pushing forward, you'll notice it stops hurting because that initial pain was more about your fearful reaction to the twist. Same goes with these new thoughts—they're like walking off a little twist of the ankle. Keep going, and the negative thoughts will subside if you keep on top of them, kicking them out and consistently replacing them. The best athletes take responsibility for their thoughts and take action to fix them to be more helpful. Direct all of your focus on doing this activity the same way you would hold your breath to get rid of the hiccups. Keep at it and don't give up.

> **Sometimes, when you feel lower than usual, trying to tell yourself,** I'm a great player *seems laughable and it won't work in the moment. Do it anyway and keep at it.*

Another great tip is to ask yourself at the moment you make a mistake: *What do I need to do now?* Focus on the answer and determine the next physical task in front of you. Allow only these thoughts and lock the door to the past.

Coach Tip:

Get your players to become their own motivators by sharing the techniques in this chapter with them. When you see a player (or the entire team) starting to fall into complacency and getting distracted by outside issues they're bringing into the dugout, ask them why they're there. Bring them back to the excitement of opening day and remind them of their goals as individuals and as a team. Positive self-talk is certainly personal, but you can share parts of it with your players. Remind them of any confidence phrases they have shared with you.

Bring them back to the excitement of opening day and remind them of their goals as individuals and as a team.

Parent Tip:

When you see your player dragging their feet with their head down after practice or a game, it usually means they are embarrassed and don't want to relive whatever they faced. Maybe they've been a bit lazy or distracted with school, and they find comfort in their mode of operating. Reject the idea of giving them a pep talk that will probably sound more like a lecture to them. Instead, be your own source of motivation and use positive self-talk to show them how to use this powerful technique. This enables you to share your experiences with them and let them manage the situation on their own.

Chapter Work-Up:

Make it a priority to learn the many ways to emphasize positives and de-emphasize negatives—exactly what the greatest athletes in the world do! Michael Jordan said, "If an opponent misses his first five shots, I can see fear in his eyes, but if I miss my first five, I think back to a game when I missed my first five and made my next ten, and I bring that confidence into this moment."

Reach back to Chapter 5 where you made your goals at the end of the chapter or look at them written on your wall or somewhere near you right now. Read them. Get out a pen and add an activity to your goals list. Make it something that's easy to do this week. Tomorrow is best. Also, ensure that it's something you can accomplish and finish that same day. All of this gets you motivated again and gives you a chance to practice positive self-talk in a different environment. Practicing positive self-talk will support your efforts.

Remember also to recognize unhelpful thoughts and kick them out, then replace them with something positive. Refocus like this until it sticks. You can be happy that you just accomplished something great. Next, you'll learn an incredibly powerful technique that will take your abilities to the next level and beyond with visualization and imagery.

PERFORMANCE JOURNAL

CHAPTER THIRTEEN

Visualization & Imagery

"If you have a clear picture in your head that something is going to happen and a clear belief that it will happen no matter what, then nothing can stop it. It is destined to happen."
—**Conor McGregor**

Before the first pitch is thrown, a game can be won or lost. Imagery is a mental skill used by many professional athletes—from Jon Lester to Tiger Woods—to sharpen their mental game. Visualizing multiple high-pressure scenarios and seeing your best moves leads to in-game confidence and improved performance. Wouldn't you like to feel more relaxed and confident going into your next game?

In this chapter, you'll learn techniques to create an imagery program that will improve your game with daily practice. You'll feel more confident while performing, slow down the game, and lower anxiety. Through patterned, consistent effort of visualization and specific imagery, you'll notice your body will comply, your muscles will react the way you want them to, and your mind will be on the ball, not the last play or the numbers on the board.

Mental imagery is seeing yourself, like a movie playing in front of you, showing the game pitch-by-pitch. The body doesn't know the difference between an imagined event and one that is real. It's why sometimes when you first fall asleep, you'll be dreaming about walking down a set of stairs and the last step drops out from under your feet, and your body jerks in response. It surprises you, right? The body will go where the mind takes it. So why not start with the mind? Let your mind process the perfect reaction by holding a practice in your mind. Then during an actual practice, your muscles will recognize the same imprint you made earlier and they will react just as you imagined it.

Mental imagery is seeing yourself, like a movie playing in front of you, showing the game pitch-by-pitch.

Your greatest opponent is always you. Mental imagery helps battle the fear of failure and insecurity that creeps into every athlete's mind at one point or another.

A Self-Guided Imagery Practice You Can Do Every Day

I have taken many athletes through guided imagery to do battle in the mind first. That way they can walk onto the field confident and ready to play the next pitch. There are several different techniques, but this is my favorite, and you can do your own guided imagery after you read this.

I have taken many athletes through guided imagery to do battle in the mind first. That way they can walk onto the field confident and ready to play the next pitch.

Lie down on your back, close your eyes, and inhale through your nose to fill your lungs and then your belly with air. Then exhale through your mouth. During the next breath in, follow the air as it enters, down your neck, along your back and chest and into your belly, relaxing your muscles along the way. Exhale out through your mouth and repeat the process two more times. Don't rush through this. You're relaxing your body so that you can focus your attention on the imagery.

Now imagine yourself out in the field, in your position, ready for the next play you want to see. Go ahead and watch plays from your last game or practice. See yourself performing and correcting the moves that need improvement. Keep yourself in this space as long as you can. If your mind drifts to a phone call you need to make, or some other distraction vies for your attention, push that thought away and head back out on the field. You need to give your all to this exercise.

See yourself performing and correcting the moves that need improvement. Keep yourself in this space as long as you can.

It helps to bring in the memories that your five senses store up for you. Remember how the ball feels in your hand, the smell of the grass, the sounds of your teammates, the taste of sweat, all of it. Let your senses guide you back into those times when you were up to bat with two outs and two strikes. Play that out in your mind and pay attention to how it feels to connect with the ball, the sound it makes, and everything you see.

Remember how the ball feels in your hand, the smell of the grass, the sounds of your teammates, the taste of sweat, all of it.

The great thing about imagery is, you can't mess it up. A daydream is imagery, and the more real it is the better, but get there however it feels best to you. The more you practice, the more vivid it will become, and the more control you'll have. Keep bringing in your five senses and run through the scenario over and over again. Imagery can be either a first-person perspective—seeing things as they will actually look to you—or a third-person perspective, like watching the scene on a movie screen in front of you. Both are good; let your natural tendency toward one be your guide and go with it.

The great thing about imagery is, you can't mess it up.

Go ahead and try the visualization exercise now. When you're done, circle the answers below that best relate to your experience:

1. While breathing and getting relaxed...

    a. I could feel my body let go, and I could see myself clearly performing what I was thinking.

    b. I was mostly relaxed; however, my mind kept interrupting the scene I was imagining with disruptive thoughts. It was hard to see myself, but I could see the game playing out in accordance with the performance I imagined.

    c. I was not relaxed, and it was hard to visualize a game. I've got a lot on my mind, and the exercise was a challenge for me.

2. When doing the breathing...

    a. My heartbeat was balanced, not too fast or too slow. I can breathe very deeply, and it feels great.

    b. My heartbeat was a bit fast, and it was kind of hard to breathe deeply. I tend to breathe sort of shallow, especially when things are tense.

    c. My heartbeat was raised, and I rushed my breathing and wondered throughout the exercise if I was doing the technique correctly.

Answers for a) **Image Ready.** Athletes who have done some meditation or guided imagery before already know how to relax their body and mind and have experience controlling their thoughts. Sometimes the environment isn't right for guided imagery, so it's best to find a place where you know that no one can interrupt you. Keep reading for more tips.

Answers for b) **Environmentally Based.** These athletes can sometimes do the imagery, and sometimes they have more difficulty. You react to your environment more quickly, and stress can distract you easily. Guided imagery is really important for you, and with daily practice, it will help you on and off the field. Keep reading for more tips.

Answers for c) **Real Life Only.** These athletes carry stress with them and are continually thinking about "what if that happens" or "when is this going to happen." You need to study and practice what you learned in Chapter 11. Take the breathing portion of the imagery practice described above and do 10-20 deep breaths. During this time, continue to push away all thoughts that have nothing to do with your vision. Be very definite and singular about what you want to replay in your mind. For example, *I'm on first base, the bases are loaded, and the pitcher is winding up.* Be strict and watch only this play out. If any other idea creeps in, kick it out immediately and get back on first base. Keep reading for more tips and keep practicing. You will get this!

Making Imagery and Visualization Work for You

Put a "do not disturb" sign on your door and get your headphones on. Even those who have experience practicing visualization and imagery can have bad days, and life throws a lot of distractions at us. These intrusive thoughts that take us off-track are your main competitors. Get them out of your head by silently "shouting" at them to go away. Then tell yourself to "stay on base" or use whatever keywords or phrases work to pull yourself back into the scenario you're playing out in your mind.

> *These intrusive thoughts that take us off-track are your main competitors. Get them out of your head by silently "shouting" at them to go away.*

Everyone is different, so you can customize the experience to make a practice that works for you. Add in relaxing music, white noise, or zero noise. Maybe try your visualizations in a dark room. Or perhaps you do your best work in the shower. Whatever it is, make it work just for you.

Find a time for doing imagery that works for you. Directly after practices or games is a good starting point. It's a great way to do a follow-up analysis of what could have been done better, and because your body was just performing those actions, everything is fresh in your mind. Pick two scenarios: one scenario in which you played perfectly and one in which you didn't hit the mark. Practice only these two in your imagery session and correct the scenario in which you messed up.

After doing a couple of these sessions, it's good to do them before performances. Be able to walk out onto the field having already been there practicing that morning. Athletes who did this reported back that they felt ready to play, leaving behind fear and insecurity and replacing them with confidence and the feeling of power.

> **Be able to walk out onto the field having already been there practicing that morning.**

Using Imagery to Combat High-Pressure Situations

Using your imagination, you can put yourself in hypothetical high-pressure situations that will alleviate the pressure of your next game.

It's the bottom of the ninth, bases loaded with two outs in the World Series as you step up to the plate. It's first-and-goal with your team down by six in the Super Bowl with only one second on the clock. It's the fifth and final round as your corner tells you that you're down four rounds to none and you need a finish to retain your championship belt. It's the final stretch in a marathon, and you have two people you need to overcome.

Seeing yourself in these situations will help acclimate your mind to a real-life high- pressure situation. Utilize positive motivation by visualizing yourself performing flawlessly in these scenarios. Tell yourself things you would want to hear if these situations were real. *The pressure is on, and I am going to come through in the clutch.* Practicing this sort of visualization with regularity will make the real situation feel like a welcome practice routine.

Reverse Visualization: Your Ticket to Less Anxiety

There is another technique called "reverse visualization" that is helpful for those who have performance anxiety. Fear of failure touches every athlete at some point in their career, and reverse visualization helps them embrace failure by imagining the worst-case scenario. By allowing yourself to be okay with making a mistake and letting the crowd make noise and letting your teammates be disappointed in you in the movie playing in your head, you overcome the fear.

By allowing yourself to be okay with making a mistake and letting the crowd make noise and letting your teammates be disappointed in you in the movie playing in your head, you overcome the fear.

So many players fail simply because their worries overtake them. They let their minds race with thoughts about mistakes that everyone else has already forgotten, and they miss the excitement of the next play that can win the game. Many players carry the burden of a mistake for weeks when the fans and teammates have long forgotten. Keep in mind that everyone is interested in the next play, the next game. Reggie Jackson struck out 2,597 times, but people don't remember that number. All they remember is watching him hit home runs. Thomas Edison famously admitted it took 1,000 failed experiments to invent the lightbulb, but all people remember to this day is his 1,001st experiment that worked.

Reggie Jackson struck out 2,597 times, but people don't remember that number. All they remember is watching him hit home runs.

To apply this technique to your pre-game (or pre-practice) routine, do the following: Get comfortable by taking a deep breath and exhaling, thinking about how every muscle in your body is letting go. Check to make sure your jaw is loose and your shoulders are down. Visualize yourself being in a situation where you feel uncomfortable and know that the feeling is going to get worse. If it makes it easier, start with the image of standing in front of an audience giving a speech, then move on to a sport situation next. Either play out the visualization as if you're watching a movie or see it first-person through your own eyes. See your teammates scowl at you and feel the embarrassment burning in your chest. Make it real, feel it, and play it out until you connect with that moment of fear, anxiety, and embarrassment. Let yourself sit with that feeling and be okay with it. Then, go ahead and correct the scene. Lift yourself up and watch yourself handle the emotions and get ready to overcome it all with an incredible performance. Tell yourself, *I got this.*

Many players struggle with performance anxiety and fear of failure, and reverse visualization helps them embrace failure and see the worst-case scenarios. Many fail because they are so worried everyone will be upset with them long-term if they fail in clutch situations. What they don't realize is that people don't remember sports failures for very long.

Michael Jordan was trusted to take the game-winning shot and failed 26 times. Nobody remembers those. They remember the 25 times he did hit the game-winning shot and definitely remember his six NBA championships.

My point is, when great athletes fail, the fans forget about it within a week, if not sooner. When they succeed in the clutch, that is what everyone remembers. Go ahead and visualize failing, feel the fans and teammates being disappointed. Let it set in, then realize that they will forget it shortly. Remind yourself there is no reason to stress and suffer from performance anxiety. After you understand that the worst-case scenarios aren't that bad, you can go back to visualizing positive situations involving proper mechanics and success. Imagery at this level can lead to amazing results.

Go ahead and visualize failing, feel the fans and teammates being disappointed. Let it set in, then realize that they will forget it shortly.

I have witnessed positive imagery help athletes recover from injuries and illness, and guide their muscles and tendons to move in more specific ways that fixed a flaw in mechanics. Players have used it to quell their anxiety, increase feelings of control, and slow down the game. This is a powerful skill that will increase in effectiveness the more you practice it and master yourself on the field.

Coach Tip:

Lead guided imagery sessions for your players as a group. Watch as your players progress on the field, staying relaxed yet powerful, as they confidently play out what they've been practicing in their minds. Encourage them to participate as a team and then remind them to do it for themselves at home post-game and pre-game. For younger players, it's best to make this part of their normal routine. When you're out in the field after a practice and gathering to review the day, go ahead and have them shut their eyes and visualize themselves going through the process of swinging the bat. Even several minutes every practice is a great start. Suggest after every practice and every game that they go to bed visualizing themselves catching fly balls and feeling confident. It's natural to want to replay what happened at practice that day, so they might as well take advantage of it and use imagery to control their physical mechanics.

Parent Tip:

Many people replay events from their day or put themselves on a beach in Hawaii as they fall asleep at night. Why not use that time and resource for creating what you want to see in order to be successful? It's been proven by elite athletes around the world that visualizing the repetition of a physical maneuver perfectly over and over again translates into real-life physical mechanics mimicking your imagery. Do it for yourself consistently for three months practicing one simple physical activity and see how it can benefit you. Be proactive about asking your athlete if they've been practicing the guided visualization at home and share your own experience using visualization with them. Creating an environment that's conducive to doing imagery and giving your athlete the tools (headphones, music, room-darkening curtains) and reminders to use them will help them make visualization a habit.

Many people replay events from their day or put themselves on a beach in Hawaii as they fall asleep at night. Why not use that time and resource for creating what you want to see in order to be successful?

Chapter Work-Up:

Maybe taking a chunk of time out of your day to lie around and watch yourself throw a ball in your mind seems too strange or even boring. You think, *I can go throw the ball with my buddy down the street instead.* But when you visualize, you are engaging your brain in this activity, letting it perfect the motions, and allowing yourself to feel calm and in control. Furthermore, this is a powerful way to "practice" when it's dark outside, when the weather is bad, when there's no one to practice with, and so forth.

The easiest way to try out visualization the first time is by doing it as soon as you go to bed. Try it tonight. You're already in the relaxed position, so you might as well use the time to replay how you looked at practice and what it felt like to perform. There is no reason not to begin using this underutilized tool that so many great athletes are using already. Get ahead of your competition and start today.

PERFORMANCE JOURNAL

CHAPTER FOURTEEN

Breathing & Relaxation

"One way to break up any kind of tension is good deep breathing."
—Byron Nelson

Of all the techniques we have covered so far, breathing and relaxation are the most like a Jedi mind trick. Government organizations, doctors, and elite athletes all teach and actively practice breathing and relaxation techniques to help them navigate intense endeavors where mistakes come at a high price. Even if the techniques you will learn in this chapter are used only for gaining an advantage over an opponent or keeping your thoughts clear for a test, it's worth every minute you practice. When your big moment comes up, you'll be ready to meet it head-on.

The Yogi and the Drill Master

We all enjoy a good underdog story, and here's one that proves there's definitely something to practicing the breathing and relaxation techniques you are about to learn, and that they pay off in sports.

Jo was a volunteer coach for a middle school soccer team in a super-competitive Southern California school system. Their team was filled with two types of athletes: Not Talented but Ambitious and Not Talented and Not Ambitious. Jo studied yoga because of some preexisting health conditions and knew how beneficial it was to breathe properly to slow down your heart rate and center your thoughts to a point of tight focus so that the noise of crowds or your own thoughts become nothing.

On the first day of practice, with expectant parents on the sidelines focusing their gaze on every word and move, Jo directed the players to close their eyes and take a breath so deep they could feel their lungs enlarge to their fullest capacity, then breathe slowly, slowly out. A player's dad shouted, "Hey, what are you doing, Coach? They need to run drills!"

After instructing the players to keep their eyes closed and focus on breathing and having no other thoughts but their breathing exercise, Jo met with the dad. "Are you good at running drills for players?" she asked. He proudly told Jo about his coaching successes in the past, let alone his own time playing on a championship team in high school. "Well, I need an assistant volunteer coach," said Jo. "You run the drills, and I'll take care of the mental part of the game before and after practice. You in?"

The dad was so worried about the team looking bad, let alone losing, that he accepted the position. According to Jo, he was amazing at setting up the drills the team needed, and they began to improve. Jo guided the athletes in yoga-based breathing techniques and calming meditation before their warm-up drills led by the other coach. It went on this way all the way up to the semi-finals.

The rag-tag team of Not Talented but now Ambitious athletes played their hearts out. They never fell to the stress and anxiety of what could be their final game. They didn't flinch or react to any mistakes they made during the game. They played in the moment. And just like that, they won, beating their Talented and Ambitious opponents. They were able to do this because they had the mentality of a predator calmly stalking its prey and attacking with confidence at the right moments, never submitting to unfocused emotions and negative thoughts.

The rag-tag team of Not Talented but now Ambitious athletes played their hearts out.

Jo also noticed that the players had amazing resilience. The goalie was kicked hard in the arm, and later found out it was fractured, but kept playing despite the pain. And this was a Not Talented and Not Ambitious player at the beginning of the season. But now this player was going up against opponents with several more years of experience. That's what positive thinking, physically demanding practices, and breathing exercises could do for a middle school soccer team. Think of what you can do with all of the techniques taught here if you practice them daily.

That's what positive thinking, physically demanding practices, and breathing exercises could do for a middle school soccer team. Think of what you can do with all of the techniques taught here if you practice them daily.

Breathing 101

Let's go over some straightforward, yet very effective techniques that professional athletes use to tackle the stressors that come with playing their sport. First up is a breathing exercise. Looking back to Jo's story, the athletes closed their eyes right there on the field, and took very purposeful breaths in through their noses and filled every bit of their lungs with air. The goalie who ended up with a fractured bone used these very breathing techniques to get through the pain.

Now, try it for yourself in the privacy of your room. Do the following for three minutes without interruption.

1. Stand up.

2. Keep your knees loosened.

3. Keep your hands hanging and relaxed at your side.

4. Close your eyes and keep them closed.

5. Direct all of your attention and thoughts to your breathing and kick out any other thoughts. Stick to it.

6. Breathe in deeply through your nose, past your chest, and down deep into your belly. Feel the air fill your lungs entirely.

7. Now, let the air out slowly through your mouth. Make sure everything is done slowly.

8. Check in with your thoughts. It helps to think quietly about every step of this process, telling yourself to relax, breathe in, and breathe out slowly. Tell yourself to go slowly and relax over and over until your timer goes off.

How do you feel? Your heart rate is down, your head is clearer, and you're more alert. You may even be able to feel the hard thump of each heartbeat. Can you imagine being in this state of relaxation and focus while playing? Many professional athletes who practice this type of breathing exercise report a supernatural slowing of time, where they can see their opponent's entire arms swing, the shift in their hips, and their eyes darting in one direction, allowing them to maneuver and position themselves to meet the challenge and overtake their opponent's attempt.

"Pressure can burst a pipe, or pressure can make a diamond."
—Robert Horry

Get Comfortable with Pressure

This last strategy ties all the other ones together. Simply put, there's no way not to feel pressured. Pressure is part of life as an athlete. Instead of trying to overcome, ignore, or fight your emotions regarding pressure, it's better to embrace it and work through it until you reach a place of balance where excitement, energy, and confidence mingle. It's okay to feel that pressure, as long as you have the mental acuity to know how to deal with it.

Eliminate the mindset that you will crumble under pressure. Instead, accept the pressure and know you will realize your goals and execute your game plan despite the pressure. Even the greatest athletes in the world experience these types of emotions, which makes Robert Horry's quote all the more relevant. The pressure is something that can knock you down and hold you back, but it's also a weapon you can utilize to your advantage.

The pressure is something that can knock you down and hold you back, but it's also a weapon you can utilize to your advantage.

Here's a technique I use with my athletes that gets you back into a space where you can think clearly and get your head back in the game.

The 4 - 7 - 8 Breath Relaxation Exercise

This simple and useful tool helps you achieve general relaxation and manage stress. Sit with your back straight. Place the tip of your tongue against the ridge of tissue behind your upper front teeth and keep it there through the exercise. Exhale through your mouth around your tongue, trying to purse your lips slightly if it seems awkward at first. Stick with this; it works. Take these counted steps next:

1. Exhale completely through your mouth, making a whoosh sound.

2. Close your mouth and inhale quietly through your nose to a mental count of 4.

3. Hold your breath for a count of 7.

4. Exhale completely through your mouth, making a whoosh sound to a count of 8.

5. This is one breath. Now inhale again and repeat the cycle three more times for a total of four breaths.

These times are just guidelines, so create your own counts if you need to. With practice, you can slow yourself down and get used to these longer times, which are helpful. This exercise will get you to the point where you can think past the pain, the anger, or the disappointment when something negative happens in your life. It's effective, and you can do it anywhere and at any time. The key is practicing it when alone just after something minorly bad happens. Then use it again during practice and build up how many times you do it during the day—the more the better. Oxygen filling your lungs and your bloodstream is medically proven to energize the body and mind, and will make your thoughts more clear.

This exercise will get you to the point where you can think past the pain, the anger, or the disappointment when something negative happens in your life.

What if you're having racing thoughts, and you can't fall asleep? Repeat the breathing technique over and over again while lying in bed. Do it again in the morning to get yourself ready for those push-ups. This breathing technique works in both scenarios—use it. And while you're at it, and you are regaining control, start using positive self-talk to insert into those relaxing blank spaces: *I'm calm, I'm good, I've got this. Breathe.*

> *While you're at it, and you are regaining control, start using positive self-talk to insert into those relaxing blank spaces:* **I'm calm, I'm good, I've got this. Breathe.**

Now that you've learned a technique to regain control and to pull yourself instantly out of a downward spiral, it's time to learn what relaxation can do for athletes when they are in control of themselves.

Relaxation Training

Gaining control of yourself and practicing what you'll be doing in the game are both extremely important to the relaxation work you will be doing next. Relaxation training pulls these factors together to enable you to react appropriately and stay in control, so you're ready for the next play, not worrying over the last play.

Here is how you can train yourself to relax, so you can tap into relaxation whenever the game gets tough. Do this at home regularly:

1. First, lie down on your back.

2. Take in a deep breath so it fills up your lungs, and you can feel it pressing into your belly. Focus on the air as it enters and leaves your abdomen, breathing out through your mouth. Do this three times.

3. Now that you've begun to relax, move through your body and tense each muscle for five seconds, starting with your toes. Going nice and slow, move through your muscles one after another, up to your forehead.

4. After the muscles have been tense for 5 seconds, release the tension and allow the body to be completely relaxed. Toes, feet, calves, quads, hamstrings, glutes, abdominals, back, pecs, fingers, hands, biceps, triceps, shoulders, mouth, forehead.

5. Finally, take a deep breath. Focus on how warm and relaxed each body part is that you just tensed and relaxed.

6. After all your muscles have let go, do some visualization in this relaxed state. Imagine

yourself making great plays in the field, at the plate, and running the bases.

7. When you're done, take time to enjoy the relaxed state you are in while maintaining focus on your breathing and the feelings in your body.

This type of relaxation method benefits you in several major ways that will improve your performances. The control you will have during high-stress moments will be magnified, and you will be able to rid yourself of unwanted tension by simply being aware of your body and by breathing the tensions out. A great bonus is that you will notice that you're able to concentrate better. All those distractions that generally take you out of the game no longer steal your attention now that you can enhance your focus and stay in the game. The power of creating vivid images of your physical mechanics, the way you play, is also enhanced. All those random thoughts and annoying memories of mistakes go quiet, so you can correct them, visualizing more clearly what your form needs to be when you play. All of this lowers your blood pressure, lowers your heart rate, and balances your breathing. This allows your body to perform at its best. You can give your full energy and attention to performing, instead of wasting energy on tight muscles and on shallow breathing that leads to bad performance.

The control you will have during high-stress moments will be magnified, and you will be able to rid yourself of unwanted tension by simply being aware of your body and by breathing the tensions out.

An excellent confidence phrase I've shared with players is: *Take a deep breath. Focus. Be present.* This puts your focus back on the present moment, where you need to be to perform your best. You can check in with yourself anytime to see if you really are in control. If not, when you feel anger or anxiety rising up inside, you now can use your breath and other tools to get present again. When you breathe out of your mouth, release all the negativity in your body and mind, and allow those deep intakes of fresh air to energize you when you're feeling sluggish. Taking a deep breath along with some positive self-talk is a great addition to your pre-pitch routine, establishing a rhythm and getting you fully in the moment.

An excellent confidence phrase I've shared with players is: Take a deep breath. Focus. Be present.

Coach Tip:

Of all the tools and techniques you can offer your players, breathing exercises have got to be the easiest. They take very little time, and they can be done anytime and anywhere without drawing attention to the player who is using them to get back in the game. All you need to do is continually remind your players to do them. Many athletes stop breathing entirely during moments of great exertion. Not only does this make for a lackluster performance, it's not healthy. Work with your players to incorporate a deep breath into their routines and have them repeat their confidence phrase quietly to themselves while doing it. Your players will be relaxed, more alert, and ready to make the next play.

Parent Tip:

Everyone experiences stressors and moments of anxiety, so chances are that you too will benefit from these breathing techniques. When combined with visualization, they are perfect for anyone to practice. The easiest way to begin is when you first climb into bed at night. (It's okay if you fall asleep while practicing.) Additionally, you can take a very deep breath and let it out in a rush through your mouth several times during the day, when stressed or just because you need a quick lift. Your adoption of these breathing techniques helps to normalize them for your athlete. If you see them getting worked up, remind them to take a deep breath. Now you can even do it with them, so they aren't alone in it.

Chapter Work-Up:

Breathing and relaxation techniques are so easy and take so little time that there's no reason not to incorporate them into your daily life. The results are immediate, and you can feel and see how they positively impact your body and mind. These are the secret weapons of so many professionals, from astronauts and fighter pilots to professional athletes. The key, like everything else in this book, is consistent practice. Right now, get out a piece of paper and write: *Take a deep breath. Focus. Be present.* Post it somewhere you can see it and enjoy taking a mindful breath anytime you need one.

PERFORMANCE JOURNAL

CHAPTER FIFTEEN

Chicken Salad

"We all face adversity throughout our lives, but with the right mindset and focus, you have the power to make all of it positive and exciting for you and those around you."

—David Angeron

Throughout my 20-plus years of coaching, my reputation as the coach who makes "chicken salad out of chicken poop" continues to grow. It is not because I am a better coach than anyone else or that I hold a certain secret to coaching. It's simply because I took the time to study sport psychology and apply it to my players and teams. It's because I got to know each of my players' personality types and coach them based on their individual mental and physical needs. And it's because I pushed them both mentally and physically to not only reach their full potential but to play above it.

It's because I pushed them both mentally and physically to not only reach their full potential but to play above it.

If you've ever seen a 5'6" pitcher stand on the mound with a look in his eyes that says he believes he's 6'5" or a 5'9" and 170-pound defensive back light up his opponents as if he's a 225-pound linebacker, then you know exactly what I mean about athletes playing above their potential. It's a mental thing; that athlete has found a way to make chicken salad out of chicken poop. It's a prime example of turning something negative like an undersized body type into something positive like an elite athlete.

My "Chicken Salad" Moment

My first real challenge as a coach came my second year coaching professional baseball. I had just been named the manager of an independent professional baseball team in Alabama. About three weeks before the start of spring training, I was called into a meeting by the league commissioner. He explained to me that the owners of the team had backed out and folded, because they were underfunded and they didn't feel like they could make a complete season of payroll and travel expenses. The team would now be taken over by the league, and the owners of the other teams in the league would fund the team to get through the season.

He then started to tell me all of the other negative ("chicken poop") problems that came along with this situation. Every other team in the league was allowed to carry a 25-man roster, but my team would be allowed only 21 players. Every other team was allowed to pay their players between $600 and $3,000 per month (based on their playing experience). All of my players could be paid only the league minimum payment of $600 per month. The other teams all had nice home stadiums, and our team would become a full-time traveling team, meaning we would play a 96-game season with all of our games being on the road. And to make matters even worse, while all the other teams got to travel on nice charter buses, our team would travel in two 15-passenger vans and use a cargo van for our equipment.

I remember sitting in that meeting with the commissioner with a nauseated feeling in my stomach. Adversity had just punched me in the throat. My team would be made up of mostly rookies straight out of college, while our opponents would have former MLB veteran players. How could we compete with that? I was faced with a choice to either turn down the job and go back to coaching high school or junior college, or keep the job and make the best out of the situation. The competitor in me decided to keep the job and get to work on a game plan to make chicken salad out of this situation.

"Mastering mental skills in sport builds momentum, making the most successful athletes and the best teams from what seemed like nothing."

—David Angeron

The first thing I did was change my goals for this team. My goals in the past have all revolved around winning. But I realized that due to the circumstances, we would struggle to compete against higher-paid veteran players. So I changed my goal to a focus on player development. This was minor league professional baseball, and I knew each of the players in the league had the same goal of advancing to higher levels. My goal was now to take these young men and develop them physically and mentally for what would definitely be a challenging season ahead of them.

My goal was now to take these young men and develop them physically and mentally for what would definitely be a challenging season ahead of them.

On the first day of spring training, I had 40 players show up, which was the league maximum for spring training. We would have two weeks to cut the group down to 21 players. The first thing I did was explain to everyone the situation about being on the road all 96 games and getting paid the league minimum. Eight players got up and walked off the field as soon as they heard this. I was down to 32 players before we picked up the first baseball. The spring training went well with team bonding routines and lots of mental and physical training drills. The tough part was deciding which 11 players I would have to cut.

The regular season consisted of a three-game series throughout the entire season, meaning we would be traveling to a different city every three days. We would have no home fans and no VIP treatment or discounts at the local restaurants and clubs like the home teams receive. Remembering that my main goal was developing the players, I hoped we could win at least one out of three games each series and not get embarrassed and swept during every series. And at the beginning of the season, that is exactly what we did, winning one of the three games in each of our first few series.

While most people expected us to struggle with the long rides in tight vans and having to stay in crappy hotels, my 21 players made the best of their experience. After all, they were playing professional baseball, so why not enjoy it? The more we played, the closer the team got and the more fun we had, which led to more positive energy. By the time we came back around to play each team for the second time, we were starting to win two out of three games and sneaking in a sweep of our own once in a while. By the time the all-star break came around, we were sitting in third place and only a few games out of first.

The more we played, the closer the team got and the more fun we had, which led to more positive energy.

As we started the second half of the season, fans from the home teams started coming to get autographs from our players. The local restaurants and clubs started giving our players the same discounts and treatment as the home players. We were being followed and interviewed by HBO and the

Chicago Tribune newspaper. This professional travel team had quickly become one of the most exciting teams to watch.

This professional travel team had quickly become one of the most exciting teams to watch.

By the end of the season, my players started to get noticed by coaches and scouts of other leagues and levels. My original goal was to help the players develop into better players and to help them advance to higher levels. When the season ended, 17 of my 21 original players advanced to play at higher levels. Three of those players who advanced (B.J. Litchfield, Andy Gros, and Bubba Dobson) can be seen on the testimonial pages at the end of this book.

My original goal was to help the players develop into better players and to help them advance to higher levels. When the season ended, 17 of my 21 original players advanced to play at higher levels.

At the beginning of that season, I remember feeling like the season was going to be a disaster. I remember fearing that it would damage my career if I didn't win. Now I look back at it as one of the most fun and rewarding seasons of my career. That season taught me not to fear situations that I cannot control. It taught me to focus on making my teams and programs so exciting that everyone wants to be a part of them. And it reinforced what I hope you will take with you forever: No matter how bad the situation is or how much "chicken poop" you are dealt, there is always a way to turn it into "chicken salad"!

CHICKEN POOP	CHICKEN SALAD
NEGATIVITY	POSITIVITY
FEAR	CONFIDENCE
ANXIETY	CALMNESS
PRESSURE	FOCUS
STRESS	SUCCESS

"Being a mental master doesn't happen just because you want it to happen. You have to learn the techniques, fuel the desire to be your best, and practice the mental side of sport with just as much commitment as the physical side."
—David Angeron

Coach Tip:

I posted a lot of other people's quotes throughout this book and offered my own quotes in this chapter, because quotes seem to have a way of inspiring us. Use the ones that you like with your players and repeat them often to keep the positive energy flowing and to help your players refocus. Though you may have been dealt a difficult team or situation, or maybe you're new to coaching and still figuring out how to lead, rest assured that you have the ability to make it fantastic. Using the mental techniques described in this book and sharing them with your players will give you that boost you need to turn what seems like a hopeless situation into a golden opportunity—to create chicken salad from what appears to be chicken poop. You can do it when you practice the techniques yourself then share them with your players.

> *Though you may have been dealt a difficult team or situation, or maybe you're new to coaching and still figuring out how to lead, rest assured that you have the ability to make it fantastic.*

Parent Tip:

Whether you're a former elite athlete or a busy parent trying to set a good example for your young athlete, you can use almost all of the tips in this book to uplift your career, life, and sport. Consistently use the breathing technique from the previous chapter (it's the easiest and most effective tool I shared) and make some goals for yourself so you can play a part in your athlete's life in sport and normalize these techniques. This shows your athlete what it looks like to make daily, consistent effort toward accomplishing goals that lead to a better way of living. Today is a great day to start if you haven't already.

> *Whether you're a former elite athlete or a busy parent trying to set a good example for your young athlete, you can use almost all of the tips in this book to uplift your career, life, and sport.*

Chapter Work-Up:

This is the most crucial chapter work-up of the entire book, so keep up your focus and energy here in the home stretch. The personal rewards you will receive because of your dedication, consistency, and hard work will make it all worthwhile.

The entire point of this book is to help you create a Mental Master Method tailor made just for you. It is based on your unique personality and circumstances, and then matched with techniques to help you reach your fullest potential. Your Mental Master Method should be used to prepare for competition, used during competition, reviewed after competition to learn what worked and what didn't, and it can even help you make a plan for moving forward.

Here's an excellent system for checking in with yourself to ensure you're in control and feel confident as you move forward. Under each of these three following sections, think of the tools, routines, and exercises that help you prepare and focus before, during, and after competition. Write down your thoughts and ideas.

Before Competition

How can I prep myself physically and mentally to connect with my talent, so I can leave everything else behind in my life and just play ball? For example, stick to your pre-game routine and post reminders of your confidence statements and positive energy statements in your bag or inside your locker. Let these remind you to take a moment to get prepared before walking onto the field. Keep your focus strong during the game using your favorite techniques from this book. Many players have in-game routines of pulling on their uniform twice or adjusting their cap while repeating their favorite positive statement. What are some of your favorite methods?

_____

_____

_____

_____

_____

During Competition

What routines, both physical and mental, can I perform to stay calm yet energized, remain focused on the moment, and play freely? For example, you might put a big red dot on your hand or write your favorite quote on your gloves—anything that will help remind you to keep your focus and allow nothing to distract you from being your best. What are your ideas?

_____

_____

_____

_____

_____

After Competition

How can I decompress and then review my actions in the game? Take the emotions out and think about what didn't work well and how you can improve it. How can you position yourself for success at the next game? What can you do at the next practice? What can you do mentally between now and then to prepare? For example, you might find a quiet place after the game—maybe that's on the ride home or in the shower—to take stock of everything and then let it go and move on to the next day. Or you might decide to never go to bed after a competition until you've reviewed the game; your job isn't finished until you've done so. You shower after a game, don't you? You need to clean up your mind as well. What are some other ways to decompress and review your actions in the game?

_____

_____

_____

_____

_____

_____

Congratulations on finishing this book and learning the skills and tools that make up your Mental Master Method! Now, go back to every chapter work-up and read over your notes. Make sure your calendar has reminders alerting you to check on your goals and to work on visualization.

Have you posted your goals and statements around your house and anywhere else that makes sense? You need reminders—we all do—so make sure yours are there and that you're reading them, practicing them, and living them every day.

There are rewards, self-confidence, and the feeling of accomplishment and pride only in work that's well done, and done often. The time has arrived for you to take everything in this book and put it to use. Now is the time to be a champion, and only you can make it happen. Get out there and be the athlete you've always dreamed of becoming today.

PERFORMANCE JOURNAL

Acknowledgments

God—First and foremost, praises and thanks to God, the Almighty, for His blessings and His will throughout my career and my research, and for helping me complete the research successfully.

My wife, Jean, my best friend and my greatest support system—I am very much thankful for her love, patience, understanding, prayers, and continued support as a coach's wife and her support to complete my research.

My children, Drake, Drew, Madeleine, and Reese, my number-one team—I know I have made my share of mistakes as a parent, like every parent does, and I will probably make several more. However, the bond and relationship I have with my four children is irreplaceable. Through the many mental and physical training sessions, to the challenging life lessons we learned together, I couldn't be more proud and grateful to have these four as my number-one team.

My parents, Ava and Dean—I am blessed and grateful to have parents who guided me and laid the foundation of preparing me for life after sports. They were my biggest fans and number-one support system. I thank them for the countless hours they put in and the sacrifices they made during my youth years as a multi-sport athlete. Nevertheless, they never let me lose sight of my priority to grow up to be a hardworking, well-mannered, and disciplined Christian man.

My siblings—I express my thanks to my brother, Chris, and to my sisters, Angie and Diana, for their support throughout the years.

Quint Studer, my mentor and inspiration—A special thank you to Quint Studer, owner of the Pensacola Blue Wahoos baseball team, who gave me my first job in professional baseball. His leadership and training helped me to become a better leader and gave me the ability to help others. His inspiration also helped me to become a better person, better husband, and better father. I credit much of my success to Quint as a mentor and a friend.

My coaches/mentors—These are coaches I played for and/or coaches I have worked with who have been positive influences in my life and who have helped pave my way to a successful career in sports. In no particular order, I would like to thank Lud Henry, John Skelton, Tim Hymel, Oliver Winston, Cooper Farris, Rick Rhodes, Joe Tueton, Dave Saunders, Bill Hamilton, Doug Martin, Tommy Minton, Chad Caillet, Al Tregle, Kash Beauchamp, and

James Gamble. I'd also like to gratefully acknowledge Tommy Bourgeois and John Menard, both of whom have passed away. Thank you both for teaching me so much.

My current and former players—Thank you to my players who put their trust and faith in me as their baseball coach, sport psychology coach, personal trainer, and college placement consultant.

Everyone who makes baseball great—Thank you to all the players, coaches (volunteers and hired coaches alike), parents, umpires, and others who devote their time and passion to baseball.

DeHart and Company Public Relations—Thanks to everyone on the DeHart and Company team who helped me so much. Special thanks to Dottie, the ever-patient manager, as well as Eve, Ashley, Anna, and everyone else in the editing, copywriting, and design team who helped make my book go from "good to great."

John Melvin Publishing—This company is named in honor of my late brother-in-law, a great athlete whom I had the honor of coaching many years ago. John, you are loved and missed.

Coach AJ Batista, Coach Jay Sanders, and Susie Farmer—Thank you for reading the early drafts of this book and helping make it better.

About the Author

David Angeron is a certified sport psychology coach who educates athletes on the mental aspects of achieving excellence in sport. More than an educator, he helps instill the lessons learned in sport and life, and guides athletes to reach their full potential.

With over 20 years of experience coaching professional, college, high school, and youth athletes, Angeron is known as an excellent motivator and a "players' coach." His years of research and implementation of sport psychology and learning to work with athletes of different personality types have enabled him to get the most out of athletes, showing them just how much more they have inside to give to their sport.

Growing up as a competitive, multi-sport athlete competing in baseball, football, soccer, basketball, and tennis tested Angeron's limits. The many mental and emotional challenges he faced during his high school years also sparked his interest in sport psychology—from getting pumped up for Friday night football games, to then rising early Saturday morning for soccer tournaments, to being reminded he was an undersized athlete and that he was too small to play college sports.

Resisting the negative and staying competitive, Angeron went on to be a two-sport athlete in college, playing both baseball and football. He credits much of his success to continually working on his mental game and bringing his unique experiences as a multi-sport athlete and professional baseball coach to his sport psychology coaching.

Angeron is founder of Mental Master Training, LLC, which specializes in mental and physical performance training for athletes. He is also the national recruiting coordinator for MyTime Sports, LLC, where he uses the network he's built through his years as a professional baseball scout to help athletes advance to college and professional sports.

David currently resides in New Orleans, LA, with his wife, Jean Melvin Angeron, and four children, Drake, Drew, Madeleine, and Reese.

Praise for David Angeron

"I started training with Coach Angeron when I was nine years old. He consistently pushed me to be mentally and physically tough. His training contributed to my confidence and my ability to perform under pressure. I greatly appreciate the time and effort that Coach Angeron dedicated to helping me become the best player I could be."

—Bryce Grizzaffi
Division I College Catcher

"I was very fortunate to be able to play for Coach Angeron in the summer of my senior year. I am a very passionate player and would sometimes let my temper and emotions get in the way of my game. Coach Angeron taught me how to control my emotions and focus all of my energy on my love and passion for competition. I have played for some great coaches, but Coach A. was one of my best motivators. His passion for helping me

control emotions and focus on positivity in both sports and life helped me become a team captain for an SEC football program. I am grateful to have him in my life as my coach and as a friend."

—Kody Schexnayder
Division I College Punter/Team Captain

"Playing for Dave was a great experience for me and my playing career. He made it clear that he was confident in my pitching ability and trusted me every day with the game on the line as his closer. Being a closer in professional baseball is a stressful and mentally challenging job. But having a coach who believed in me and truly understood the importance of being able to 'get in the zone and stay in the zone' was a valuable benefit to me and my professional career."

—B.J. Litchfield
Closer, Pensacola Pelicans Professional Baseball

"I am grateful for the opportunity to play for Coach Angeron and the 2018 'Cinderella Team,' the Westgate High School Tigers. When Coach took over the team, Westgate was a group of mentally weak individuals who would fold under pressure and get angry when we faced adversity with other teams, umpires, or fans. Coach Angeron taught us a lot about the game of baseball, but the mental discipline he demanded of us was what changed our season and the lives of many players on that team. When many players and fans had started to give up on the season, Coach A. continued to believe

in us and continued to teach us how to focus and manage our emotions. He transformed our team from being mentally weak individuals to becoming a mentally tough team. That is how the Westgate Tigers became the first #31 ranked team to ever reach the Louisiana State Tournament."

—Michael Sonn
NAIA College Outfielder

"*I was blessed to be raised in a family that instilled mental and physical toughness training into our daily lives. In September of my high school junior football season, I tore my ACL. While others doubted that I would be able to participate in my junior baseball season, I was back on the baseball field four months after my ACL surgery. Playing through the pain with a knee brace on was difficult at times, but my resilience paid off as we won the state championship that season. The mental toughness training that my dad taught me all my life was the only thing that kept me going and gave me the ability to overcome adversity and continue my playing career.*"

—Drake Angeron
Division II College Centerfielder

"*I was fortunate to be able to play for Dave in the summer before college and then again in professional baseball following my college career. What mental toughness means to me...it's when you put on your jersey and you become fearless, unbreakable, and unbeatable because you know that there is no possible way your opponent prepared harder than you. It's staying humble and knowing that you are not the best, but you can beat the best. It's having confidence, but being your worst critic. It's wanting the ball all of the time and wanting the ball, even more, when your team is the underdog. It is when you credit your team for the win and blame yourself for the loss. That is what leaders do. It's when you win a game 2-1 and you are not satisfied because you gave up that one run. It's when you throw a shutout and you are still not satisfied because you gave up a walk. It's when you look in the mirror and you are honest with yourself on what you need to improve on. Just like your physical game, there is always room for improvement in your mental game as well. I greatly appreciate Coach Dave for the guidance and faith in me while helping me to achieve my goals.*

—Andy Gros
Division I College LHP All-American;
Starting Pitcher, Pensacola Pelicans
Professional Baseball

"I am grateful and was very fortunate to play for Dave to start my professional career. It was a great experience getting to sit and talk with Dave about all aspects of the game. Dave was a players' coach and knew when to be all business, but also knew when to have fun. Dave expected you to be at your best every time you laced up your spikes, mentally and physically. Being mentally tough is a big part of playing baseball or just life itself. If things don't go your way, or you just don't have your best stuff that day, you must dig deep

and trust your ability to make plays or make a pitch. You must play pitch to pitch, play to play, and one at-bat at a time. You cannot let one bad pitch get you off your game plan. Baseball is a game of failure, and it will humble you quickly, but it is how you come back from being knocked down that counts the most. You cannot let your emotions show no matter what the situation is. The key is 'being able to get in the zone and stay in the zone.' You must act like that's what you expected to happen and move on to the next pitch. As a pitcher, being mentally tough is a must. You have to play the game like you're 6'5"/230 lbs. while knowing that you are the best player on the field every time your number gets called. Dave was very good at getting players to play at their full potential for him, and I am thankful that I was able to experience his love and passion for the game."

—Bubba Dobson
Pitcher, Southeastern Cloverleafs &
Pensacola Pelicans Professional Baseball

"Coach Angeron wasn't just any normal coach walking around the field. The mentorship he gave me was like nothing I had ever experienced in my life. He never questioned my physical ability, but he questioned my mental toughness. He always said how you perform in crunch time will not be determined physically but mentally. Coach Angeron broke it down for me on why mental toughness was so important. I didn't realize it at that moment, but once I joined the United States Army, it all came together. The army broke me down physically, so

the only thing I had left was the mental toughness that had been instilled in me by Coach Angeron. Being mentally weak in the military can cost lives on the battlefield, and I can't thank Dave Angeron enough for making me mentally stronger. One thing he always said that stuck with me was, 'Being mentally strong will come to use in every aspect of life, not just sports.' Coach Angeron couldn't have been more correct with that statement."

—Drake Granier
Former Ellender Memorial High School
Athlete & Current U.S. Army Staff
Sergeant

Another Book from David Angeron

Understanding College Recruiting and College Placement

IT'S MY TIME

James L. Gamble & David L. Angeron
WWW.MYTIMESPORTS.COM

How to Make Your College Recruitment Dream a Reality—One Small Choice at a Time

The competition is fierce. The process is intense. And there's plenty of misinformation flying around that could potentially derail your efforts. All of these factors can feel overwhelming to young athletes hoping to be recruited (not to mention their parents and coaches).

David Angeron and James Gamble are here to help. Drawing on their firsthand experience and their "inside view" from playing, coaching, and working as Major League Baseball scouts, they've distilled their most helpful advice in this tactical guidebook. Readers will learn:

- The four qualities of athletes who make it past high school baseball (Hint: mental toughness counts for more than you think!)
- How to maximize your use of the NCAA's Eligibility Center
- Tips for leveraging your academic strengths to boost your GPA
- What to do before your campus visit to make a powerful impression on coaches
- Why your social media presence can make or break scholarship opportunities
- How to choose the best camps and showcases for you
- High-impact ways to invest your time and money into your recruitment journey
- The difference between committing and signing
- Common myths about college baseball success (and how not to fall for them!)

It's the small choices you make every day that over time add up to success. This book helps you create a best-odds plan for developing your talents, connecting with the right people, making the best decisions at the right time—and ending up on the team of your dreams. David Angeron and James Gamble don't just teach it; they've lived it.

Both have played college baseball and worked as Major League Baseball scouts. David is the founder of Mental Master Training, LLC. James is the founder of the Global Scouting Bureau. They combine their talents to help athletes, parents, and coaches understand college recruiting and placement practices, providing the players who are the future of baseball a clear path to success.

To learn more or to order the book, visit www.mytimesports.com.

About MyTime Sports

MyTime Sports is one of the most credible college placement services in the country. Trusted by over 1,600 college baseball coaches, 800 college softball coaches, and 500 college basketball coaches, MyTime Sports places players in all levels of colleges across the country. MyTime Sports also provides opportunities for advancement to professional sports through our large network of independent and international professional leagues.

Eliminating human error with our Flightscope Analytics equipment and having experienced professional scouts help provide the most accurate data and recruiting information to college coaches from coast to coast. Join our Prospect Placement Plan today (visit www.mytimesports.com for pricing). It will change your life!

Want to help your entire team or every player in your organization get exposure to college coaches and professional scouts? Be sure to check out our team/organization rates.

EDUCATION, EVALUATION, EXPOSURE

Education

MyTime Sports advisors assist players and their families in understanding every aspect of the recruiting process. This education maximizes their recruiting offers and helps to avoid costly mistakes due to the common myths surrounding baseball recruiting. Our goal is to provide accurate information to help our prospects make the best decisions to fit their athletic and educational needs. Our advisors are available to our prospects 24/7 via call, text, or email.

Evaluation

Our professional scouts personally evaluate each prospect's transferrable tools, academics, videos, mechanics, and overall future potential to accurately promote them to the correct level for their optimal chances of success. We are not here to pad anyone's ego. Our job is to provide accurate evaluations to the college coaches. The MyTime Sports network and reputation have been built on credibility and honest evaluations from our 20+ years of professional scouting experience. Our Flightscope Analytics technology is the most accurate and reliable source of measuring transferrable tools.

Exposure

MyTime Sports actively pursues the perfect fit for each of our prospects. Unlike many other companies that create a player profile that sits statically on a recruiting website—and college coaches have to pay a membership fee in order to view your profile—MyTime Sports creates profiles that are available to *all* college coaches for free. We also actively communicate with college coaches daily through our personal relationships with thousands of college coaches via cell phone calls, text, and email.

If you're ready to take the next step in pursuing your goals, please contact:

David Angeron, National Recruiting Coordinator
Email: mail@mytimesports.com
Phone: 504-345-9566
www.mytimesports.com

Made in the USA
Middletown, DE
25 February 2022